Assessing L2 Digital Multimodal Composing Competence

This book focuses on assessing L2 student digital multimodal composing (DMC) competence. It explores key themes, including the conceptualization of L2 student DMC competence, and the development, validation, and utilization of L2 student DMC competence in the tertiary context.

Through a thorough review of the DMC literature, the book furnishes readers with a theoretical framework to comprehensively grasp the underlying constructs of L2 student DMC competence. It also provides a delineation of the process of scale development, i.e., defining constructs, constructing items, and analyzing items, scale validation, i.e., the structural, external, and consequential construct validity of the scale, and scale utilization in students' DMC self- and peer-assessment practices.

This practical guidance equips educators and practitioners with the necessary tools and strategies to effectively assess and enhance L2 students' DMC competence. Scholars and professionals in the fields of L2 writing, language assessment, digital literacy, and technology-enhanced language learning will gain valuable insights from the content.

Emily Di Zhang received her Ph.D. degree from the Faculty of Education, University of Macau. She is Postdoctoral Fellow in the School of Foreign Languages, Shanghai Jiao Tong University, Shanghai, China. Her research interests include technology-mediated language learning, teaching, and assessment. She has publications in journals like *Computer Assisted Language Learning*, *Journal of Second Language Writing*, *System*, *Language Teaching Research*, *Assessing Writing*, *Applied Linguistics Review*, *Language Assessment Quarterly*, and *Innovation in Language Learning and Teaching*. She is a reviewer for journals such as *Journal of Second Language Writing*, *Assessing Writing*, *Applied Linguistics Review*, and *The Asia-Pacific Education Researcher*.

Shulin Yu is Associate Professor at the Faculty of Education, University of Macau. His research interests include L2 writing, and classroom feedback and assessment in higher education. His publications have appeared in *Educational Research Review*, *Assessing Writing*, *Journal of Second Language Writing*, *Language Teaching Research*, *Language Teaching*, and *TESOL Quarterly*. He is listed among the top 2% of scientists in a global ranking released by Stanford University. The ranking identifies the top 2% among seven million scientists by citations, H-index and HM-index for 2020–2023 and over one's career. He is Associate Editor of *Journal of Second Language Writing*, *Assessing Writing*, and *The Asia-Pacific Education Researcher*, and Guest Editor of Special Issues for *The Asia-Pacific Education Researcher*, and *Assessing Writing*.

Routledge Focus on Applied Linguistics

Discourses of Borders and the Nation
A Discourse-Historical Analysis
Massimiliano Demata

Health Disparities and the Applied Linguist
Maricel G. Santos, Rachel Showstack, Glenn Martínez, Drew Colcher, Dalia Magaña

Instruction Giving in Online Language Lessons
A Multimodal (Inter)action Analysis
Müge Satar and Ciara R. Wigham

Language Policy and the Future of Europe
A Conversation with Seán Ó Riain
Alice Leal and Seán Ó Riain

Creative Metaphor, Emotion and Evaluation in Conversations about Work
Jeannette Littlemore, Sarah Turner and Penelope Tuck

Assessing L2 Digital Multimodal Composing Competence
Emily Di Zhang and Shulin Yu

For more information about this series, please visit: www.routledge.com/Routledge-Focus-on-Applied-Linguistics/book-series/RFAL

Assessing L2 Digital Multimodal Composing Competence

Emily Di Zhang and Shulin Yu

LONDON AND NEW YORK

First published 2024
by Routledge
4 Park Square, Milton Park, Abingdon, Oxon OX14 4RN

and by Routledge
605 Third Avenue, New York, NY 10158

Routledge is an imprint of the Taylor & Francis Group, an informa business

© 2024 Emily Di Zhang and Shulin Yu

The right of Emily Di Zhang and Shulin Yu to be identified as authors of this work has been asserted in accordance with sections 77 and 78 of the Copyright, Designs and Patents Act 1988.

All rights reserved. No part of this book may be reprinted or reproduced or utilised in any form or by any electronic, mechanical, or other means, now known or hereafter invented, including photocopying and recording, or in any information storage or retrieval system, without permission in writing from the publishers.

Trademark notice: Product or corporate names may be trademarks or registered trademarks, and are used only for identification and explanation without intent to infringe.

British Library Cataloguing-in-Publication Data
A catalogue record for this book is available from the British Library

ISBN: 9781032758077 (hbk)
ISBN: 9781032758084 (pbk)
ISBN: 9781003475729 (ebk)

DOI: 10.4324/9781003475729

Typeset in Times New Roman
by Newgen Publishing UK

Contents

List of figures		*viii*
List of tables		*x*
Preface		*xi*
Acknowledgments		*xiii*
About this Book		*xiv*
1	Assessing digital multimodal composing competence	1
2	Conceptualizing and modelling L2 student digital multimodal composing competence	12
3	Scale development for assessing L2 student digital multimodal composing competence	45
4	Scale validation for assessing L2 student digital multimodal composing competence	57
5	Scale utilization for assessing L2 student digital multimodal composing competence	90
6	Conclusion	107
	Index	*115*

Figures

2.1	The interrelationships between Available Design, Design, and the Redesigned	16
2.2	A model of L2 student DMC competence	17
2.3	A ten-point holistic scale for DMC performance assessment	19
2.4	The use of texts, pictures, and animations in Yijie's group work	22
2.5	The utilization of multiple modes in Jingjing's group work	23
2.6	The bilingual captions in Jingjing's group work	25
2.7	Alice, the flower-planting woman, and bloopers	26
2.8	The painting and paper cutting in Sisi's group work	27
2.9	The self-painting in Anastasia's group	28
2.10	Cheng's group work on dishonesty	29
2.11	The concurrent relationship of modes in Siqi's group work	32
2.12	The complementary relationship of modes in Siqi's group work	33
2.13	Wen's group work about a game character's travel	35
3.1	The processes of developing the L2 student DMC competence scale	46
4.1	The first-order five-factor 20-item model	60
4.2	The first-order four-factor 15-item model	62
4.3	The second-order four-factor 15-item model	63
4.4	Infit and outfit statistics of *cohesion of modes*	64
4.5	Infit and outfit statistics of *genre awareness*	64
4.6	Infit and outfit statistics of *language use*	64

4.7	Infit and outfit statistics of *digital skills*	65
4.8	Category probability curves for *cohesion of modes*	65
4.9	Category probability curves for *genre awareness*	66
4.10	Category probability curves for *language use*	66
4.11	Category probability curves for *digital skills*	67
4.12	Mia's writing sample on the roommate relationship	77
4.13	The use of statistics in Christina's second essay	78
4.14	The rating scale for the IELTS writing task	80
5.1	The four-second pause in the DMC work	95
5.2	The feedback report generated by *Pigai* for Emma's group's script	96
5.3	Humorous elements in Rachel's DMC group work	99
5.4	The genre of speech in Allen's DMC group work	99

Tables

3.1	The first version of the L2 student DMC competence scale	50
3.2	Factor loadings and variances of the 20-item L2 student DMC competence scale	52
3.3	The EFA-generated L2 student DMC competence scale	54
4.1	The final version of the L2 student DMC competence scale	63
4.2	The scale dimensions and reliability indices	67
4.3	Correlations between L2 student DMC competence and L2 proficiency	70
4.4	Descriptive statistics of L2 proficiency scores	73
4.5	Correlation matrix between DMCs over time	73
4.6	Correlation matrix between MWs over time	73
4.7	Results of the parallel process model (PPM)	75
5.1	The DMC self-assessment sheet	91
5.2	The DMC peer-assessment sheet	93

Preface

In the post-pandemic digital and generative AI age, how we communicate has shifted dramatically from paper to screen, and thus multimodality has become the normal state of contemporary communication. Digital multimodal composing (DMC), as a technology-enhanced task in L2 writing, pertains to a textual practice that leverages digital tools to create texts by orchestrating various semiotic modes, including linguistic, auditory, visual, gestural, and spatial modes. Despite a recent proliferation of research on the instructional designs of DMC projects and the learning potentials and affordances for L2 students, one area that remains relatively unexplored is the assessment of L2 student competence in DMC, which can be defined as the knowledge, skills, and attitudes necessary for designing L2 DMC artifacts. While a plethora of research has endeavoured to elaborate instructional designs for DMC and its affordances for L2 students, limited research attention has been given to the measurement of L2 student DMC competence. Many L2 professionals and teachers have struggled to find effective ways to measure students' multimodal competence. This book focuses on assessing L2 student DMC competence, and its main themes include conceptualization of L2 student DMC competence, scale development, scale validation, and scale utilization of L2 student DMC competence in the tertiary context.

Through a comprehensive exploration of DMC assessment, the book offers a theoretical foundation for understanding L2 student DMC competence. This theoretical grounding enables readers to obtain a comprehensive understanding of the underlying constructs of L2 student DMC competence. It delineates the process of scale development, including defining constructs, item development, and refinement. The book provides a detailed account of scale validation, including the gathering of structural, external, and consequential construct validity evidence. It also explores the utilization of the scale in L2 students' self- and peer-assessment practices in an assessment as learning (AaL) focused L2 classroom. This book offers methodologies and examples that can be applied in real-world contexts. This practical guidance equips educators and practitioners with the necessary tools and strategies to effectively assess and enhance L2 students' DMC competence.

This book differentiates itself from existing literature through its innovative approach to assessing L2 student DMC competence. It goes beyond previous works by taking an etic approach to conceptualize L2 student DMC competence via analyzing effective DMC samples, and it takes both etic and emic approaches to capturing L2 student DMC competence by analyzing effective DMC samples, student focus group interviews, and classroom observations. It also throws light on the process of scale development and validation, marshalling structural, external, and consequential construct validity evidence for the scale, making it a robust tool to use. The book goes further to explore L2 students' scale-referenced self- and peer-assessment processes in a naturalistic L2 classroom setting, providing important insights into the use of the scale as an AaL tool.

Acknowledgments

We first and foremost extend our sincerest thanks to the participants in the research. This book would have been impossible without their active participation and great efforts in the DMC projects and their insightful perspectives in the research on DMC competence. We also owe a debt of gratitude to the four reviewers of this book. They recognized its unique value and provided us with constructive comments for the content.

Chapter 2 is derived from an article published in *Computer Assisted Language Learning*. Chapter 3 and Chapter 4 are based on an article published in *Computer Assisted Language Learning*. Chapter 5 stems partially from an article published in *System*.

About this Book

While a plethora of research has endeavoured to elaborate instructional designs for DMC and its affordances for L2 students, little attention has been paid to assessing L2 student DMC competence. Many L2 professionals and teachers have struggled to assess students' multimodal composing competence. To address the research gaps, the present study sought to develop, validate, and utilize an L2 student DMC competence scale in the L2 classroom.

Drawing on the multiliteracies and multimodality theories, the empirical studies of L2 student DMC competence, and the data of the present study from student focus group interviews, classroom observations of student self- and peer-assessment, and DMC sample analysis, a model of L2 student DMC competence was proposed. Based on this conceptualization, the L2 student DMC competence scale was constructed and then validated. Exploratory factor analysis (EFA) was conducted to analyze the items, and items that were not meaningful and interpretable were eliminated. The structural construct validity of the scale was examined by performing confirmatory factor analysis (CFA) based on students' self-reported DMC competence against the scale. The external construct validity of the scale was inspected by performing correlation analysis between DMC competence and L2 proficiency measured by an L2 test, and latent growth curve modelling (LGCM) analysis between DMC competence and L2 monomodal writing competence measured by L2 writing tasks. The consequential construct validity of the scale was examined based on student interviews about the effect of the scale on their monomodal writing. Students' utilization of the scale in self-assessment practices was explored through student interviews, classroom observation of self- and peer-feedback, and DMC sample analysis.

The findings led to the proposal of a multidimensional construct of L2 student DMC competence, based on which a 45-item scale was drafted. In terms of the structural construct validity of the scale, CFA indicated that the first-order four-factor 15-item model had the best model fit. As for the external construct validity, correlation analysis indicated that DMC competence was significantly correlated with L2 proficiency. LGCM analyses suggested that DMC competence co-developed with monomodal writing competence. Regarding the consequential construct validity, student interviews showed that the scale had a positive washback effect on students' print-based L2 writing. The scale played an important role in students' self-assessment processes, and students of differing L2 proficiency exhibited different features in using the scale in the DMC self-assessment practices partly due to their goal orientations.

This study addresses one of the most difficult and pressing issues in DMC research, i.e., DMC assessment, and is significant in shedding light on the construct of L2 student DMC competence, providing a robust instrument to assess DMC projects, and facilitating L2 students to use the scale to set their goals, monitor their progress, reflect on their strengths and weaknesses, and ultimately improve their multiliteracies and multimodal writing competence.

1 Assessing digital multimodal composing competence

Digital multimodal composing in L2 contexts

In the post-pandemic digital and generative artificial intelligence (GAI) age, how we communicate has shifted dramatically from paper to screen (Belcher, 2017; Kress, 2003, 2010; Shin et al., 2021), and thus multimodality has evolved into the prevailing mode of contemporary communication (Belcher, 2017; Bateman, 2014; Kress, 2003, 2010). As one crucial communicative act, writing no longer relies on "language" as the sole carrier of meaning, which becomes one means among many (Grapin, 2019; Kress, 2010). Conventional literacy, which primarily focuses on the linguistic mode, seems inadequate for L2 learners to address the demands of meaning representation and communication in the digital age. Writers who lack proficiency in digital reading and writing, particularly in conjunction with media utilization, may be at a disadvantage (Belcher, 2017). L2 learners need a new literacy for the comprehension and composition of multimodal texts to effectively express ideas, establish connections, and portray identities in their daily lives (Buckingham, 2008; Kafai & Peppler, 2011). Simultaneously, the incorporation of technology into language teaching and learning has been a discernibly rising trend, with pervasive evidence of its normalization (Bax, 2003; Moorhouse et al., 2023; Moorhouse & Kohnke, 2021). Virtually all educational endeavours are now facilitated through digital technologies, marking a significant shift in instructional methodologies (Elola & Oskoz, 2017; Godwin-Jones, 2023; Moorhouse, 2020; Moorhouse et al., 2023). Consequently, L2 learners are progressively immersing themselves in the utilization of a plethora of digital tools and engaging with diverse multimodal learning materials and texts (Yi et al., 2020).

DOI: 10.4324/9781003475729-1

2 Assessing DMC competence

In light of the recent advancements in GAI, there is a prospective expansion in opportunities for language learning and multimodal writing (Bibauw et al., 2022; Godwin-Jones, 2023; Liu et al., 2024). This development poses the potential for both unprecedented advantages and challenges within the realm of L2 writing (Barrot, 2023; Yan, 2023). As such, there has been a persistent call for researchers to direct their attention towards the consideration of multimodality in L2 writing (Casanave, 2016; Hirvela & Belcher, 2016; Li, 2021; Yi, 2017). In this context, there is a noteworthy upsurge of interest to be observed in the domain of digital multimodal composing (DMC) among scholars and educators specializing in L2 writing across a spectrum of educational settings (e.g., Park, 2021; Jiang, 2017; Jiang & Luk, 2016). DMC, as a technology-enhanced task in L2 writing, pertains to a textual practice that leverages digital tools to create texts by orchestrating various semiotic modes, including linguistic, auditory, visual, gestural, and spatial modes (Jiang, 2017; New London Group, 1996). This practice spans various genres, such as graphic novels, academic posters, video essays, illustrated books, pamphlets, PowerPoint presentations, video documentaries, web pages, memes, and infographics, to name just a few (Hafner & Ho, 2020; Jiang, 2017; Li & Pham, 2022; Ryu et al., 2022; Yang, 2012; Zhang & Yu, 2023a). Empirical research documents that DMC holds the potential to offer students various advantages, including heightening semiotic awareness (Nelson, 2006), facilitating identity construction (Honeyford, 2014; Yi & Hirvela, 2010), enhancing individual authorial voice (Hafner, 2014; Hepple et al., 2014; Kim & Li, 2021), increasing motivation in general L2 learning and L2 writing (Hafner & Miller, 2011; Jiang & Luk, 2016; Kim & Vorobel, 2017; Koohang et al., 2009; Neo & Neo, 2010), sharpening the ability to express emotions (Kim & Li, 2021; Yang & Wu, 2012), honing critical thinking skills (Yang & Wu, 2012), and enhancing genre and audience awareness (Cimasko & Shin, 2017).

Despite a recent proliferation of research on the instructional designs of DMC projects and DMC's learning potentials and affordances for L2 students, one area that remains relatively unexplored is the assessment of L2 student competence in DMC (Belcher, 2017; Deng et al., 2023; Yi et al., 2017; Yi et al., 2020; Zhang et al., 2021), which can be defined as the knowledge, skills, and attitudes necessary for designing L2 DMC artifacts. Assessment, a crucial component of the learning process, plays a vital role in promoting collaborative and participatory learning (Carless, 2009; Jin, 2022; Johnson & Johnson, 1999). DMC differs fundamentally from traditional monomodal print-based writing, as it involves the orchestration of multiple modes in meaning making. Therefore, assessing DMC competence needs to capture both linguistic and non-linguistic elements (Jiang et al., 2019; Mills & Exley, 2014). Additionally, it is vital to identify valid criteria and indicators of learning during DMC activities (Wyatt-Smith & Kimber, 2009) to help teachers assess students' current levels of DMC competence, gather evidence of learning during and after participation in DMC projects, and gauge the effectiveness of DMC instruction.

Of the existing instruments that measure L2 DMC, some scales capture one specific trait of DMC competence: Hung et al.'s (2012) rating scale to assess L2 students' multimodal compositions focuses on *cohesion of the various modes*. Likewise, Fajardo's (2019) scale gauges L2 students' DMC performance by highlighting how visual-linguistic and audio-visual modes are cohesively leveraged.

Other scales encompass different features of DMC competence. For example, Dzekoe's (2017) DMC scale includes *context, substance, organization*, and *style: language and use*. *Context* refers to whether the topics are original, thoughtful, and audience engaging. *Substance* pertains to whether the content is relevant, appropriate, and rich. *Organization* denotes whether the thesis is explicit, the idea is presented logically, the main idea is present, and the transitions are used effectively. *Style: language and use* focuses on whether the language is correct and appropriate and whether academic English is used properly. In the DMC scale of Lee et al. (2019), the criteria encompass *language use* in terms of fluency, accuracy, and style that is suitable for the audiences' needs, *text-image composition* regarding the complementarity between texts and images, and *authenticity and uniqueness* concerning whether new meaning is made using self-selected modes or by reshaping the available modes. Li (2020) created a more fine-grained rating scale to assess students' DMC performance, which includes *content, technology, graphic design, language and mechanics*, and *creativity*. *Content* concerns the presentation of content on the relevant topics and the demonstration of content knowledge. *Technology* refers to the effective deployment of digital tools and technology affordances for communication. *Graphic design* pertains to the effective combination of multiple modes for message communication and audience engagement. *Substance* pertains to whether the content is relevant, appropriate, and rich. *Language and mechanics* represents accurate grammar, usage, and mechanics. *Creativity* involves the creative leveraging of multiple modes and knowledge representation. While this rating scale expands the understanding of DMC competence, it is specifically applied to a content course, i.e., Teaching English to Speakers of Other Languages (TESOL) teacher education, and content knowledge representation might be less irrelevant to other courses. In a similar vein, Kim et al. (2022) employ their self-created rating scale to assess L2 student DMC performance through *task fulfillment, content, organization, language & mechanics*, and *effectiveness of using multi-modes*. *Task fulfillment* refers to the presence of summary, arguments, and conclusion. *Content* represents the presence of a well-developed storyline and a clear main idea with relevant and sufficient supporting ideas and details. The storyline only applies to narratives and is irrelevant in argumentations or expositions. The presence of clear main ideas and supporting ideas and details relate more to *organization*. *Organization* describes the structures of writing and the consistency of viewpoints and focus. *Language & mechanics* represents the mastery of English and standard English conventions. *Effectiveness of using multi-modes* refers to the effective exploitation of modes to support writing.

Considering the genre of DMC, Elola and Oskoz (2022) designed a scale for digital stories, which includes the criteria of *audience, oral narration, music/sound effects, visuals, grammar, vocabulary,* and *multilingual and translingual practices*. *Audience* concerns audience engagement; *oral narration* refers to the clarity of narration; *music/sound effects* pertains to the complementary role of a soundtrack for narration; *visuals* represents the clarity of images; *grammar* refers to a wide range of L2 grammatical structures with few or minor errors; *vocabulary* refers to making full use of the L2 vocabulary about the topic; and *multilingual and translingual practices* concerns making excellent use of several linguistic repertoires in a coherent manner. Likewise, Ryu et al. (2022) developed a scale to assess L2 students' DMC performance in their meme project, and it consists of *multimodality, cultural aspects, linguistic components,* and *task/functions*. *Multimodality* pertains to the utilization of multiple modes and cohesion of modes. *Cultural aspects* concerns the effective employment of cultural knowledge. *Linguistic components* describes the effective use of linguistic knowledge. *Task/functions* relates to the demonstration of genre-specific features of the memes. As this scale applies specifically to memes as a transmission unit of culture

(Dawkins, 2006), the *culture* dimension might not generalize to other DMC projects.

A perusal of the existing scales reveals that while they have captured important aspects of DMC works, there is a notable lack of consistency across these scales. Different researchers have emphasized various dimensions of DMC competence, a divergence primarily attributed to the elusive nature of the construct of L2 student DMC competence, being conceptualized by the etic approach of analyzing effective DMC samples or teacher perceptions of student DMC competence. In addition, the existing scales tend to be product-oriented, and are employed by teachers to assess the end products of DMC artifacts and fall short of identifying the students' cognitive and metacognitive activities throughout the DMC project. Scales that comprehensively cover the crucial aspects of DMC competence are rare, making it challenging to precisely evaluate students' DMC competence and identify weaknesses in their DMC skills.

Secondly, the instruments designed to assess L2 student competence in DMC lack rigorous validation (e.g., Dzekoe, 2017; Hung et al., 2012; Jiang et al., 2022; Ryu et al., 2022). The lack of the marshalling of validity evidence might give rise to misleading inferences and interpretations of students' DMC competence levels.

Thirdly, the existing instruments for measuring DMC competence have predominantly been employed by teachers as assessment of learning (AoL) tools, which are typically utilized at the end of an L2 DMC project. However, DMC, as a technology-enhanced L2 writing task, presents students with new opportunities to engage in self- and peer-assessment. They can, for example, review their own voiceovers and make revisions if they are unsatisfied with their pronunciation. They may also iteratively review their scripts to rectify grammatical and lexical errors or seek peer feedback to help them identify linguistic mistakes. Despite ongoing calls to implement assessment as learning (AaL) in L2 writing instruction (Earl, 2013; Lee, 2017), there is a paucity of scales to employ as self- or peer-assessment tools in DMC projects to cultivate students' metacognition of their DMC competence.

Objectives and aims of this book

To bridge the research gaps identified, the initial research objective of this book was to form a comprehensive understanding of L2 student

DMC competence by taking both etic and emic approaches. Drawing from relevant theories, such as multiliteracies and multimodality, extant empirical research on L2 student DMC competence, and data gathered through student focus group interviews, classroom observations, and DMC samples, a model for L2 student DMC competence was conceptualized, which served as the foundation for the development of the L2 student DMC competence scale.

The second objective of this research was to validate the scale for measuring L2 student DMC competence. This validation process was guided by Messick's (1995) construct validity framework and involved a thorough examination of the scale's structural, external, and consequential construct validity. The structural construct validity was examined by conducting confirmatory factor analysis (CFA) to determine whether students' self-reported L2 student DMC competence scores align with the internal structure of the scale. The external construct validity was evaluated through correlation analysis, which analyzed the relationship between L2 students' DMC competence scores and their performance in L2 proficiency tests. Additionally, latent growth curve modelling (LGCM) was performed to analyze the dynamic interplay between L2 student DMC competence and L2 monomodal writing competence. The consequential construct validity was explored by analyzing student interviews, focusing on their perceptions of how using the L2 DMC scale affected the development of their traditional print-based L2 monomodal writing skills.

The third objective of this research was to implement the scale and inspect its impact on students' self- and peer-assessment practices in the context of DMC projects. Data were gathered from student interviews, classroom observations, DMC samples, and teacher reflections. This triangulation of data sources increased the trustworthiness of the findings and facilitated a thorough investigation into the utilization of the scale and its impact on students' self- and peer-assessment practices in DMC projects.

Outline of the book

Chapter 1 serves as an introduction to the book, providing the background and rationale for assessing L2 student DMC competence. It outlines the research objectives that the book aims to address and provides an overview of the book's scope and organization.

Chapter 2 sketches out the theoretical frameworks relevant to assessing L2 student DMC competence. It discusses various theoretical perspectives from multiliteracies and multimodality that inform the assessment of L2 student DMC competence. Furthermore, it proposes a theoretical model for conceptualizing L2 student DMC competence based on theoretical perspectives, empirical findings in the literature, and the data from this research.

Chapter 3 focuses on the development of an assessment scale for measuring L2 student DMC competence. It defines the constructs underpinning the scale based on the proposed DMC competence model in Chapter 2. The chapter elaborates on the processes of defining constructs, constructing items, analyzing items, and the iterative process of refining the scale.

Chapter 4 explores the validation of the assessment scale for L2 student DMC competence. It depicts the validity framework and approaches relevant to the scale, including the structural, external, and consequential construct validity. The chapter delineates the collection and analysis of the validity evidence for the scale, including CFA, correlation, and LGCM analyses.

Chapter 5 focuses on the practical implementation and utilization of the assessment scale in classroom contexts. It explores how the L2 student DMC competence scale can be effectively used as a self- and peer-assessment tool in DMC projects and how the teacher can reflect on the use of the scale in an AaL-focused classroom.

Chapter 6 provides a summary of the key findings discussed throughout the book. It highlights the implications of the research findings for future research directions and practical applications in assessing L2 writing. The chapter concludes with closing remarks, reflecting on the significance and contribution of the book to the field of L2 writing and its implications for L2 writing pedagogy.

References

Barrot, J. S. (2023). Using ChatGPT for second language writing: Pitfalls and potentials. *Assessing Writing, 57*, 100745.

Bateman, J. (2014). *Text and image: A critical introduction to the visual/verbal divide*. Routledge.

Bax, S. (2003). CALL: Past, present, and future. *System, 31*(1), 13–28.

Belcher, D. D. (2017). On becoming facilitators of multimodal composing and digital design. *Journal of Second Language Writing, 38*, 80–85.

Bibauw, S., François, T., Van den Noortgate, W., & Desmet, P. (2022). Dialogue systems for language learning: A meta-analysis. *Language Learning & Technology, 26*(1), 1–24. Buckingham, D. (Ed.). (2008). *Youth, identity, and digital media.* MIT Press.

Carless, D. (2009). Trust, distrust and their impact on assessment reform. *Assessment & Evaluation in Higher Education, 34*(1), 79–89.

Casanave, C. P. (2016). Qualitative inquiry in L2 writing. In R. M. Manchón & P. K. Matsuda (Eds.), *The handbook of second and foreign language writing* (pp. 497–517). de Gruyter.

Cimasko, T., & Shin, D. (2017). Multimodal resemiotization and authorial agency in an L2 writing classroom. *Written Communication, 34*(4), 387–413.

Dawkins, R. (2006). *The selfish gene* (4th ed.). Oxford University Press.

Deng, Y., Liu, D., & Feng, D. (2023). Students' perceptions of peer review for assessing digital multimodal composing: the case of a discipline-specific English course. *Assessment & Evaluation in Higher Education.* Advance online publication.

Dzekoe, R. (2017). Computer-based multimodal composing activities, self-revision, and L2 acquisition through writing. *Language Learning & Technology, 21*(2), 73–95.

Earl, L. M. (2013). *Assessment as learning: Using classroom assessment to maximize student learning.* Corwin Press.

Elola, I., & Oskoz, A. (2017). Writing with 21st century social tools in the L2 classroom: New literacies, genres, and writing practices. *Journal of Second Language Writing, 36*, 52–60.

Elola, I., & Oskoz, A. (2022). Reexamining feedback on L2 digital writing. *Studies in Second Language Learning and Teaching, 12*(4), 575–595.

Fajardo, M. F. (2019). Cohesion and tension in tertiary students' digital compositions: Implications for teaching and assessment of multimodal compositions. In H. S. Joyce & S. Feez (Eds.), *Multimodality across classrooms: Learning about and through different modalities* (pp. 178–193). Routledge.

Godwin-Jones, R. (2023). Emerging spaces for language learning: AI bots, ambient intelligence, and the metaverse. *Language Learning & Technology, 27*(2), 6–27.

Grapin, S. (2019). Multimodality in the new content standards era: Implications for English learners. *TESOL Quarterly, 53*(1), 30–55.

Hafner, C. A. (2014). Embedding digital literacies in English language teaching: Students' digital video projects as multimodal ensembles. *TESOL Quarterly, 48*, 655–685.

Hafner, C., & Miller, L. (2011). Fostering learner autonomy in English for science: A collaborative digital video project in a technological learning environment. *Language Learning & Technology, 15*(3), 68–86.

Hepple, E., Sockhill, M., Tan, A., & Alford, J. (2014). Multiliteracies pedagogy: Creating claymations with adolescent, post-beginner English language learners. *Journal of Adolescent & Adult Literacy, 58*(3), 219–229.

Hirvela, A., & Belcher, D. (2016). Reading/writing and speaking/writing connections: The advantages of multimodal pedagogy. In R. M. Manchón & P. K. Matsuda (Eds.), *The handbook of second and foreign language writing* (pp. 587–612). de Gruyter.

Honeyford, M. (2014). From aquí and allá: Symbolic convergence in the multimodal literacy practices of adolescent immigrant students. *Journal of Literacy Research, 46*(2), 194–233.

Hung, H.-T., Chiu, Y.-C. J., & Yeh, H.-C. (2012). Multimodal assessment of and for learning: A theory-driven design rubric. *British Journal of Educational Technology, 44*(3), 400–409.

Jiang, L. (2017). The affordances of digital multimodal composing for EFL learning. *ELT Journal, 71*(4), 413–422.

Jiang, L., & Luk, J. (2016). Multimodal composing as a learning activity in English classrooms: Inquiring into the sources of its motivational capacity. *System, 59*, 1–11.

Jiang, L. & Ren, W. (2020). Digital multimodal composing in L2 learning: Ideologies and impact. *Journal of Language, Identity & Education, 20*(3), 167–182.

Jiang, L., Yu, S., & Lee, I. (2022). Developing a genre-based model for assessing digital multimodal composing in second language writing: Integrating theory with practice. *Journal of Second Language Writing, 57*, 100869.

Jiang, L., Yu, S., & Zhao, Y. (2019). Teacher engagement with digital multimodal composing in a Chinese tertiary EFL curriculum. *Language Teaching Research, 25*(4), 613–632.

Jin, Y. (2022). Test-taker insights for language assessment policies and practices. *Language Testing, 40*(1), 193–203.

Johnson, D. W., & Johnson, R. T. (1999). Cooperative learning and assessment. In D. Kluge, S. McGuire, D. Johnson, & R. Johnson (Eds.), *JALT applied materials: Cooperative learning* (pp. 164–178). Japan Association for Language Teaching.

Kafai, Y. B., & Peppler, K. A. (2011). Youth, technology, and DIY: Developing participatory competencies in creative media production. *Review of Research in Education, 35*, 89–119.

Kim, D., & Li, M. (2021). Digital storytelling: Facilitating learning and identity development. *Journal of Computers in Education, 8*(1), 33–61.

Kim, D., & Vorobel, O. (2017). Discourse communities: From origin to social media. In: S. Wortham, D. Kim & S. May (Eds.), *Encyclopedia of Education: Volume 3, Discourse and Education* (pp. 267–282). Springer.

Kim, Y., Kang, S., Nam, Y., & Skalicky, S. (2022). Peer interaction, writing proficiency, and the quality of collaborative digital multimodal composing task: Comparing guided and unguided planning. *System, 106*(4), 102722.

Koohang, A., Riley, L., Smith, T., & Schreurs, J. (2009). E-learning and constructivism: from theory to application. *Interdisciplinary Journal of Knowledge and Learning Objects, 5,* 91–109.

Kress, G. (2003). *Literacy in the new media age.* Routledge.

Kress, G. (2010). *Multimodality: A social semiotic approach to contemporary communication.* Routledge.

Lee, I. (2017). *Classroom writing assessment and feedback in L2 school contexts.* Springer.

Lee, S-Y, Lo, Y-H, & Chin, T-C. (2019). Practicing multiliteracies to enhance EFL learners' meaning making process and language development: a multimodal problem-based approach. *Computer Assisted Language Learning, 34*(1–2), 66–91.

Li, M. (2020). Multimodal pedagogy in TESOL teacher education: Students' perspectives. *System, 94,* 102337.

Li, M. (2021). *Researching and teaching second language writing in the digital age.* Palgrave Macmillan.

Li, M., & Pham, Q. N. (2022). Three heads are better than one? Digital multimodal composition completed collaboratively versus individually. *Language Teaching Research.* Advance online publication.

Liu, M., Zhang, L. J., & Biebricher, C. (2024). Investigating students' cognitive processes in generative AI-assisted digital multimodal composing and traditional writing. *Computers & Education, 211,* 104977.

Messick, S. (1995). Validity of psychological assessment: Validation of inferences from persons' responses and performances as scientific inquiry into score meaning. *American Psychologist, 50,* 741–749.

Mills, K. A., & Exley, B. (2014). Time, space, and text in the elementary school digital writing classroom. *Written Communication, 31*(4), 434–469.

Moorhouse, B. L. (2020). Adaptations to a face-to-face initial teacher education course 'forced' online due to the COVID-19 pandemic. *Journal of Education for Teaching, 46*(4), 609–611.

Moorhouse, B. L., & Kohnke, L. (2021). Responses of the English-language-teaching community to the COVID-19 pandemic. *RELC Journal, 52*(3), 359–378.

Moorhouse, B. L., Wong, K. M., & Li, L. (2023). Teaching with technology in the post-pandemic digital age: Technological normalisation and AI-induced disruptions. *RELC Journal, 54*(2), 311–320.

Nelson, M. E. (2006). Mode, meaning, and synaesthesia in multimedia L2 writing. *Language, Learning, & Technology, 19*(2), 56–76.

Neo, M., & Neo, T. K. (2010). Students' perceptions in developing a multimedia project within a constructivist learning environment: A Malaysian experience. *The Turkish Online Journal of Educational Technology, 9*(1), 176–184.

New London Group. (1996). A pedagogy of multiliteracies: Designing social futures. *Harvard Educational Review, 66*(1), 60–92.

Park, J. H. (2021). "Dear future me": Connecting college L2 writers' literacy paths to an envisioned future self through a multimodal project. In D. Shin, T. Cimasko, & Y. Yi (Eds.), *Multimodal composing in K-16 ESL and EFL education: Multilingual perspectives* (pp. 73–86). Springer.

Ryu, J., Kim, Y. A., Eum, S., Park, S., Chun, S., & Yang, S. (2022). The assessment of memes as digital multimodal composition in L2 classrooms. *Journal of Second Language Writing, 57*, 100914.

Shin, D., Cimasko, T., & Yi. Y. (2021). *Multimodal composing in K-16 ESL and EFL education*. Springer.

Smith, B. E., Pacheco, M. B., & Khorosheva, M. (2020). Emergent bilingual students and digital multimodal composition: A systematic review of research in secondary classrooms. *Reading Research Quarterly, 56*(1), 33–52.

Wyatt-Smith, C., & Kimber, K. (2009). Working multimodally: Challenges for assessment. *English Teaching: Practice and Critique, 8*(3), 70–90.

Yan, D. (2023). Impact of ChatGPT on learners in a L2 writing practicum: An exploratory investigation. *Education and Information Technologies*. Advance online publication.

Yang, Y. F. (2012). Multimodal composing in digital storytelling. *Computers and Composition, 29*, 221–238.

Yang, Y. F., & Wu, W. I. (2012). Digital storytelling for enhancing student academic achievement, critical thinking, and learning motivation: A year-long experimental study. *Computers & Education, 59*(2), 339–352.

Yi, Y. (2017). Establishing multimodal literacy research in the field of L2 writing: Let's move the field forward. *Journal of Second Language Writing, 38*(4), 90–91.

Yi, Y., & Hirvela, A. (2010). Technology and 'self-sponsored' writing: A case study of a young Korean American. *Computers and Composition, 27*(2), 94–111.

Yi, Y., King, N., & Safriani, A. (2017). Reconceptualizing assessment for digital multimodal literacy. *TESOL Journal, 8*(4), 878–885.

Yi, Y., Shin, D., & Cimasko, T. (2020). Special issue: Multimodal composing in multilingual learning and teaching contexts. *Journal of Second Language Writing, 47*, 100717.

Zhang, E. D., & Yu, S. (2023a). Implementing digital multimodal composing in L2 writing instruction: A focus on developing L2 student writers. *Innovation in Language Learning and Teaching, 17*(4), 769–777.

Zhang, M., Akoto, M., & Li, M. (2021). Digital multimodal composing in post-secondary L2 settings: a review of the empirical landscape. *Computer Assisted Language Learning, 36*(4), 694–721.

2 Conceptualizing and modelling L2 student digital multimodal composing competence

Introduction

Despite a substantial body of studies on the instructional design and affordances of DMC for L2 learners (e.g., Cimasko & Shin, 2017; Hafner, 2014; Nelson, 2006; Yi & Hirvela, 2010), limited attention has been given to the conceptual models and frameworks of DMC competence, which are prerequisites for L2 learners to successfully design DMC works and respond to the multimodal reading and writing demands of the digital era. Informed by previous research and theories (e.g., Hafner & Ho, 2020; Jiang, 2017), DMC competence can be defined as the set of knowledge, skills, and attitudes required when designing L2 DMC works. Unaware of what constitutes DMC competence, researchers lack the theoretical basis to develop instruments to measure L2 student DMC competence. In addition, L2 teachers grapple with determining what to teach and what to assess (Hafner & Ho, 2020; McKee & DeVoss, 2013; Yi et al., 2017) for DMC projects, and they tend to refer to print-based L2 writing in teaching and assessing DMC (Hava, 2021; Jiang et al., 2019; Lee et al., 2019; Oskoz & Elola, 2016), and neglect the distinctions between multimodal and monomodal writing.

Previous empirical studies on L2 student DMC competence have focused on the salient features of L2 student DMC competence through DMC sample analysis (e.g., Hafner, 2014; King, 2021; Smith et al., 2021; Wang, 2008), and teachers' perceptions of L2 student DMC competence through interviews (Hafner & Ho, 2020). They have primarily taken an etic approach to capturing DMC competence from the perspective of researchers or teachers who did not themselves design DMC works, and few have taken an emic approach to

DOI: 10.4324/9781003475729-2

eliciting perceptions of DMC competence from L2 learners who have first-hand participatory experience of designing DMC works.

Hence, to address this research gap, and building on earlier findings about DMC competence in the literature, this chapter aims to take an emic approach to developing a conceptual model of DMC competence. It first briefly sketches out the two dominant theoretical frameworks in multimodal composing studies in TESOL and applied linguistics (i.e., multiliteracies and multimodality). The authors then propose an L2 student DMC competence model based on empirical data from L2 learners who have participated in DMC projects, gathered from student focus group interviews, classroom observations of student self- and peer assessment in the DMC projects, and DMC sample analysis.

Theoretical rationale for DMC

Multimodality

The meaning of texts is no longer solely determined by their written language because of the shift in representational and communicational mediums from page-based to screen-based media brought about by digital technology (Shin & Cimasko, 2008); rather, meaning is jointly constructed by the language mode and other semiotic modes (Kress, 2000). According to Kress (2003) and O'Halloran & Smith (2013), multimodality is the process of conveying meaning using a variety of modes, including both digital and non-digital forms. Mode is defined as "a socially shaped and culturally given resource for meaning making" (Kress, 2017, p. 60). Modes fall into linguistic, visual, audio, gestural, and spatial modes (Shin & Cimasko, 2008). Different modes possess different affordances, i.e., functional specializations (Kress, 2010). For instance, speech and writing share the function of naming; images are germane for depiction; and gestures have the function of enacting, indicating, emphasizing, and sketching out topics or themes. Layout can position semiotic elements and their relations and orient viewers/readers to classifications of knowledge, such as "centrality" or "marginality" and "given" or "new".

The orchestration of several semiotic modes to produce multimodal ensembles is described by multimodality theory (Kress, 2010). Earlier researchers have extensively discussed the text-image relationship (or verbal-visual relationship). For instance, Barthes (1977) highlighted the interplay between texts and images in conveying meaning and interpretation. Key concepts related to this topic are "anchorage" and "relay". Anchorage refers to the way texts can be used to guide or direct the interpretation of images. That is, texts can serve as an anchor, providing context, explanation, or clarification for the meaning of the accompanying images, which enable viewers/readers to understand the intended message or interpretation of the images. Relay involves a more complex interaction between texts and images, where both contribute to the overall meaning but do not duplicate each other's content. They work together to create a more nuanced or layered interpretation, where the texts and images complement each other, providing different facets of the message. Kloepfer (1977) (cited from Bateman, 2014) extended this account beyond Barthes' ideas: Whereas Barthes merely focused on cases where texts and images pull in the same direction, Kloepfer added a "divergent" relationship, referring to cases where texts and images make opposite meanings. In cases where texts and images do work convergently, they are further classified based on whether the texts and images are additive or parallel. The additive relationship includes "amplifying" and "modifying". The former concerns one strengthening the other, being synonymous with "relay" in Barthes (1977), while the second involves one changing the other by adding some details or specifications (Bateman, 2014), corresponding to "anchorage" in Barthes (1977). Building on such earlier ideas, Jones and Hafner (2012) and Unsworth (2008) postulated that semiotic modes can relate to one another in three different ways: concurrency, in which their meanings support one another; complementarity, in which they have different meanings but still support one another; and divergence, in which their meanings conflict in order to produce particular effects, such as humour or irony. For the representation and communication of meaning, students can orchestrate multiple modes concurrently, complementarily, or divergently.

To deliver their intended meanings, meaning makers shape and reshape ways of presenting messages, and thus transformation and transduction are pivotal actions when designing multimodal artifacts (Kress, 2003). Transformation refers to the procedures by which semiotic resources are reordered and repositioned within one mode. Although the procedure is important, there is no ontological change because it involves the same entities. All syntagms, texts, and semiotic objects can be transformed. Transduction involves reorganizing semiotic resources across modes. Each mode has a unique materiality and a variety of entities: e.g., speech has words, whereas images do not. In order to complete the process of transduction, meaning must be rearticulated from the entities of one mode into the entities of the new mode: e.g., from speech to texts, or from texts to images.

In DMC, students leverage multiple semiotic modes in representing and communicating meanings, and take advantage of the different affordances of different modes to realize specific functions. They may organize modes concurrently, complementarily, or divergently to make their intended meanings. They also need to reorder or reorganize available modes within or across modes to deliver their messages.

Multiliteracies

According to Fairclough (1995), the multiliteracies theory reinterprets literacy as the orchestration of numerous semiotic modes to create multimodal ensembles in various genres. The ensembles create new meanings by imaginatively representing, contextualizing, and transforming the existing modes (New London Group, 1996). Meaning makers reimagine themselves as they create multimodal ensembles by rebuilding and renegotiating their identities (New London Group, 1996).

According to the multiliteracies theory (Barton & Hamilton, 1998; New London Group, 1996), literacy is more of a socially situated activity in the context of literacy events than a collection of cognitive skills in individual minds. As distinct literacy events specify various contexts with various social purposes, requiring various discursive forms (i.e., genres, registers, and styles), literacy is multiple and multifaceted. Learning to coordinate multimodal semiotic resources in a range of social contexts is a necessary component of developing literacy. It also entails appropriating genres, registers, and styles, as well as "ways of acting, interacting, feeling, believing, valuing, and using various sorts of objects, symbols, tools, and technologies — to recognize yourself and others as meaning and meaningful in certain ways" (Gee, 2005, p. 7). In order to appropriate discursive forms, one must either draw on textual choices to create presentations of one's self while playing various roles in various social contexts that involve audiences, purposes, and media, or one must appropriate social identities made available by the discourse to demonstrate affiliation to specific discourse communities.

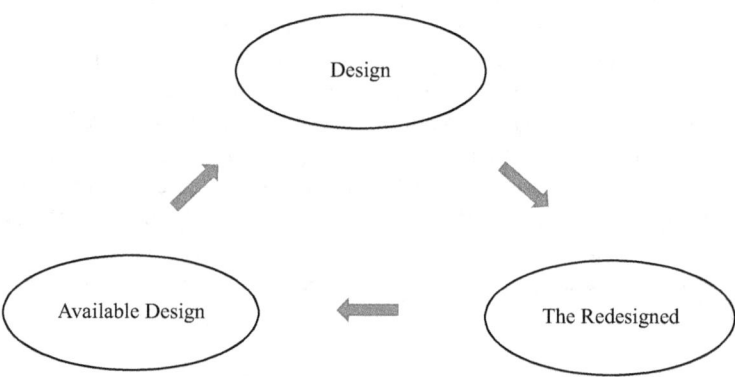

Figure 2.1 The interrelationships between Available Design, Design, and the Redesigned.

According to the New London Group (1996), new literacy practice is a design process that includes Available Design, Design, and the Redesigned. Available Design refers to the elements of design that are verbal, visual, aural, gestural, and spatial. Design requires the depiction, recontextualization, and transformation of Available Design to create new meaning rather than a simple replication or reproduction of Available Design or recombination of Available Design elements. The result of Design is the Redesigned, which then reemerges as new Available Design. Figure 2.1 illustrates the connections between Available Design, Design, and the Redesigned.

Situated within the multiliteracies theory, DMC is defined as a new literacy practice in which students utilize the new medium, i.e., digital technologies, and draw on multiple Available Designs, such as linguistic, visual, audio, gestural, and spatial modes, to Design the orchestration of the modes and form the Redesigned, i.e., multimodal artifacts. Meanwhile, they appropriate genres, registers, and styles to construct their identities and address target audiences. They can use the Redesigned artifacts to recreate Available Designs.

Conceptualizing and modelling L2 student DMC competence

While the multimodality and multiliteracies theories offer valuable insights into comprehending DMC as a literary practice, there

DMC competence conceptualization 17

has been a scarcity of frameworks proposed to conceptualize DMC competence, which is the basis for the assessment of students' DMC projects. Based on empirical data from student focus group interviews, classroom observations, and DMC sample analyses in the mainland Chinese L2 classroom (Zhang & Yu, 2023b), we propose our own L2 student DMC competence model (see Figure 2.2). As shown in the model, DMC competence is a multifaceted concept encompassing a number of dimensions including the *utilization of multiple modes*, *genre awareness* (including the aspect of *audience awareness*), *digital skills*, *creativity*, *delivery*, *cohesion*, *identity expression*, *language use* (including the aspect of *linguistic choices*), and *organization*.

In the sections that follow, we first present how the model was developed from a research project aiming to investigate the DMC

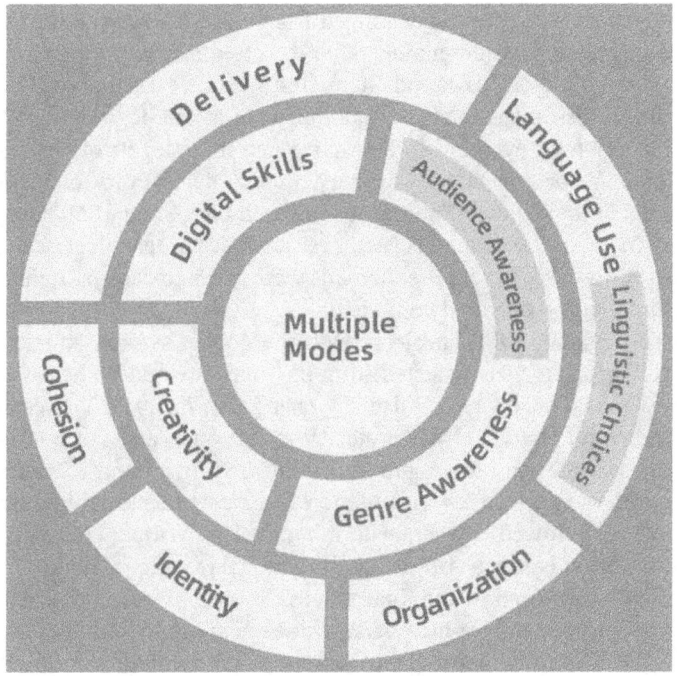

Figure 2.2 A model of L2 student DMC competence.

Note: "Multiple Modes" represents "Utilization of Multiple Modes"; "Cohesion" represents "Cohesion of Modes"; "Identity" represents "Identity Expression".

competence utilized by Chinese L2 learners in their DMC projects. Then we provide a detailed introduction to our model and elaborate on its significance and implications for assessing DMC in L2 contexts.

Development of the model of L2 student DMC competence

The model was developed from a qualitative research project that was carried out at a university in mainland China where all undergraduate students who do not major in English are required to take an English course. The goals of the course are to help Chinese students become more proficient in all aspects of English, including speaking, listening, reading, writing, and translating. This course included a total of 64 sessions throughout the semester, two sessions a day, two days a week. The DMC project was utilized in the classroom as a writing task. A total of 200 first-year university students from four full classes of the College English I course agreed to take part in the research project. Their ages ranged from 18 to 23 years. All of these students were pursuing majors other than English, including Arts, Art and Technology, Music, and Computer Science. Based on the scores of an English assessment test administered at the beginning of their university journey, they were grouped into three levels of classes: A, B, and C. For our study, we focused on students from four B-level classes of the College English course, each consisting of 50 students. The first author was the instructor responsible for teaching these four classes. In the research, pseudonyms were given to each participant to ensure their privacy and confidentiality.

To align the DMC projects with the course syllabus, the topics for the projects were selected from the units covered in the textbook "New Horizon College English" by Zheng (2017a, 2017b). The choice of genre for the L2 DMC project was left open and not restricted. In accordance with the approach outlined by Jiang and Ren (2020), the project involved a series of steps: Students began with textbook reading, followed by brainstorming, script-writing, filming, the collection and creation of various multimodal resources, video editing, and the production of the final videos. Students were organized into groups of three to five members, with each group tasked with producing DMC works that ranged from two to five minutes in duration. These works were designed to leverage multiple semiotic modes, including audio, video, music, text, images, and gestures, based on the group's specific goals and interests. The instructor facilitated the

DMC competence conceptualization   19

process by providing training to students on creating L2 DMC works. This training involved introducing various modes, offering examples, and providing guidance on video editing tools. Once the projects were completed, students presented their works in class, offering self-assessments and providing feedback on their peers' projects. The instructor employed a holistic grading scale with ten points to assess the overall quality of the DMC samples (refer to Figure 2.3 for details). The students needed to design three DMC artifacts over the semester, which accounted for ten percent of their final grade for the course.

Data were collected from three sources: (1) Student focus group interviews, (2) classroom observations of student self- and peer- feedback sessions, and (3) DMC samples. With regard to the focus group interviews, we employed a purposive sampling approach to select ten groups, consisting of a total of 44 students, who had achieved Excellent scores (ranging from 9 to 10 points) on the DMC project. The rationale for choosing them was twofold: First, their exemplary samples were likely to exhibit a range of effective DMC characteristics, thereby providing insights into relevant DMC competencies; and second, these students were expected to demonstrate more extensive and frequent application of DMC competence. The first author initiated the interviews by offering a thorough clarification of the terms used, with a particular focus on the dimensions of L2 DMC competence, as derived from the existing literature. Subsequently, the interview protocol (see Appendix) was followed to inquire about whether and how the students utilized any of these dimensions of L2 DMC competence when creating their DMC projects, as well as whether and how they incorporated additional competencies throughout the process. During the interviews, equal attention was paid to each participant within the group, in line with Yin's (2016) approach. Throughout the interviews, the researcher adhered to established principles of

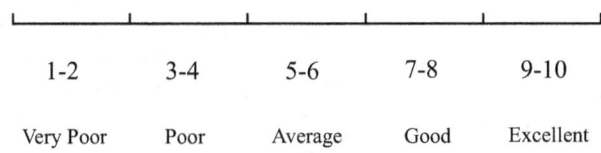

Figure 2.3 A ten-point holistic scale for DMC performance assessment.

effective interviewing, which included strategies such as limiting the amount of speech, adopting a non-directive approach, maintaining a neutral stance, establishing rapport with participants, following an interview protocol, and engaging in ongoing analysis during the interview process (Yin, 2016). All interviews were recorded in audio format and then transcribed verbatim for subsequent analysis.

In terms of the classroom observations, following the completion of the DMC project, four class sessions were set aside for students to present their DMC samples and orally comment on both their own and their classmates' group works. Observations were made while the students were conducting self- and peer-assessment. As observation data can be directly seen with the eyes and perceived with the senses, observation is a useful way to collect naturalistic data (Yin, 2016). Students were required to first comment on the positives and negatives of each group's work after viewing it. Subsequently, they were asked to articulate the advantages and disadvantages of their respective group works. The instructor recorded the students' oral comments and took note of the essential points that they raised.

In addition, as a supplementary data source, all students' DMC samples were collected for the nature of the details they contained (Yin, 2016). Document analysis is often used in combination with other qualitative research methods as a means of triangulation, that is, to seek convergence and corroboration by using different data sources and methods (Denzin, 1970; Jick, 1979; Yin, 2016) and "a confluence of evidence that breeds credibility" (Eisner, 1991, p. 110). The more convergence there is, the stronger the evidence is. The DMC samples were reviewed by the researcher ahead of the interviews for the purposes of (1) avoiding interrupting an otherwise healthy flow of conversation by asking the participants about the content of the DMC samples, such as the title and topic of the samples, and (2) determining important features of L2 student DMC competence and providing a contextualized understanding of L2 student DMC competence.

For data analysis, the transcripts from the student focus group interviews and classroom observations were subjected to manual coding, guided by the established coding scheme for L2 student DMC competence. This scheme was developed based on prior scholarly works (e.g., Cimasko & Shin, 2017; Hafner, 2014; Hafner & Ho, 2020; King, 2021; Kress, 2003, 2010; New London Group, 1996; Park, 2021). Deductive coding techniques were employed during data analysis (Yin, 2016). We were also open to any relevant aspects of L2

DMC competence, including insights not explicitly addressed in the literature (Mackey & Gass, 2005). Common and significant themes were identified to determine the specific aspects of L2 DMC competence utilized by the students. To enhance the reliability of the data analysis process, the first author and a second coder, a Ph.D. student in Applied Linguistics from a mainland Chinese university, initially coded half of the data independently. The intercoder reliability coefficient was calculated at 0.858. Any discrepancies in coding were resolved through discussions to reach a consensus. Subsequently, the primary researcher independently coded the remaining half of the data. Triangulation of data from multiple sources was employed to enhance the reliability and validity of the analysis. Furthermore, member checking was conducted by sharing the research findings with participants to validate the accuracy of the data analysis and interpretation.

Figure 2.2 presents a visual representation of L2 student DMC competence as it is currently understood. It consolidates various dimensions identified through theoretical and empirical literature, as well as the data from this chapter, and presents them within a multilayered donut chart. The outer circle encompasses *delivery, language use, organization, identity expression*, and *cohesion of modes*, all of which can be indicative of the quality of DMC products. It is worth noting that *linguistic choices* are included as a subcategory of *language use*, as L2 learners adjusted their language choices based on the selected genres. The middle circle includes *digital skills, genre awareness* (with *audience awareness* as a sub-dimension), and *creativity*, which are integral to L2 learners' DMC competence during the process of designing their DMC works. These dimensions interact with one another. For instance, *delivery* surrounds *digital skills* and *audience awareness*, as the adjustment of captions and dubbing in *delivery* relies on video editing skills, and the primary purpose of delivering DMC works fluently is to make sure that the audience comprehends and engages with the content. *Language use* is linked to *genre awareness* and *audience awareness* because different genres necessitate distinct linguistic styles, and L2 learners need to use language that is comprehensible, empathetic, interesting, and humorous to interact effectively with their audience. *Genre awareness* is positioned between *organization* and *identity expression*, as different DMC genres require different organizational structures and may showcase varying identities. *Creativity* is positioned between *cohesion of modes* and *identity expression* because

22 DMC competence conceptualization

the combination of modes and the construction of desirable identities in self-designed stories both involve creative elements. At the core of this model is the *utilization of multiple modes*, serving as the foundation upon which all other dimensions of DMC competence are built.

The dimensions of L2 student DMC competence

Utilization of multiple modes

Utilization of multiple modes refers to how L2 learners incorporate various modes into their DMC projects. These modes encompass elements such as texts, images, colour, layout, videos, music, sounds, animation, and role-plays, as outlined in the works of scholars like Kress (2003, 2017) and the New London Group (1996). During the interviews, all participants consistently emphasized that they made extensive use of multiple modes to enhance the content of their L2 DMC projects. For instance, Yijie explained that they developed the script by consulting relevant internet essays (i.e., texts). They also employed their original drawings (i.e., images), which they subsequently transformed into animations. This was further confirmed through the analysis of DMC samples, which revealed the presence of texts, images, and animations in Yijie's group project (see Figure 2.4).

Jingjing similarly mentioned her efforts to incorporate multiple modes into her project, encompassing sound effects, music, texts, role-plays, and videos, with the aim of effectively conveying her concepts related to digital life. This was substantiated through the analysis of her group's work samples, where various modes were indeed

Figure 2.4 The use of texts, pictures, and animations in Yijie's group work.

Figure 2.5 The utilization of multiple modes in Jingjing's group work.

present (refer to Figure 2.5 for details). What is more, during classroom observations where students provided feedback on their own projects, Jingjing emphasized her deliberate use of multiple modes as a means of providing supporting evidence for her argument that digital life has both positive and negative aspects.

Utilization of multiple modes stands out as a fundamental aspect of DMC competence, serving as both a defining characteristic of DMC works and a prominent feature demonstrated in this chapter. This finding aligns with prior research, which also identified the incorporation of various modes such as texts, images, colour, videos, music, soundtrack, animation, and layout in DMC works as means to convey meaning (Hafner, 2014; Oskoz & Elola, 2016; Smith et al., 2021; Tardy, 2005; Wang, 2008).

Genre awareness

Genre awareness refers to the deliberate use of language and organizational structures tailored to different genres to fulfil specific intentions and address particular audiences, as emphasized by scholars such as Hafner and Ho (2020) and Jiang et al. (2022). In the interviews with participants from seven groups, it became evident that they employed distinct languages and organizations for various genres of DMC works, each serving unique purposes. For instance, when working within the narrative genre, Sisi's group explained that their aim was to convey a story about the encounter between an ancient individual and a modern one, highlighting the contrast between ancient and modern life through dialogues. They employed an oral and humorous language style and organized their work chronologically to narrate the story. An examination of their DMC sample supported these characteristics, revealing the use of emotional terms like "amazing", "nice", "awesome", and "interesting", as well as a more subjective tone compared to argumentative or expository genres. Sunny's group, also within the narrative genre, shared their intention to depict a story about a girl who faced challenges but eventually excelled in her new major. Despite the somewhat serious topic, they aimed for a fun tone, employing an informal and casual language style. Like Sisi's group, they utilized a chronological organizational structure, which was evident in their DMC sample.

In contrast, for the argumentative genre, Siqi's group exemplified how students consider linguistic choices to effectively present their argument "that money needs to be spent in accordance with financial situations". They emphasized the need for a serious and formal language style, frequently using expressions like "in our opinion" and "we believe" to convey their arguments. They acknowledged the importance of logic in persuasion, reflecting their awareness of using language that is appropriate for certain genres. The sample analysis confirmed the formal and logical language style, replete with expressions indicating their stance.

Anastasia's group, focusing on the exposition genre, aimed to inform the audience about digital life. They consciously maintained an objective, formal, and expert-like language style, as they were presenting factual information. Their organizational structure followed a cause-effect pattern, aligning with their goal. The sample analysis confirmed the formal and objective language style, as well as the cause-effect organizational structure.

Additionally, Xinyi's group disclosed their deliberate use of lengthy and intricate sentence structures, along with a diverse and complex vocabulary, to project professionalism, richness, and informativeness. They adhered to the problem-solution pattern, being consistent with the sample analysis.

Genre awareness was readily evident in the DMC works produced by the students, where distinctive linguistic styles and organizational structures were employed to match the various DMC genres, each intended for specific purposes and audiences. For instance, when creating narratives aimed at storytelling and audience engagement, the students utilized informal and subjective linguistic styles, as well as chronological organizational structures. On the other hand, when crafting argumentative pieces designed for persuasion, they adopted formal, objective, and logical linguistic styles, along with the traditional thesis structure of statement-evidence-conclusion. Similarly, for informative content, such as expository works, they favoured objective language styles and structured their compositions using cause-effect and problem-solution formats. These findings meshed well with King (2021), which observed the use of different languages in public service announcements and hip-hop music videos, and Smith et al. (2021), which noted the distinct language patterns used in the reflective genre of L2 DMC, including causal reasoning, evidence appraisal, and comparison and contrast.

Audience awareness, a subcategory of *genre awareness*, pertains to L2 learners' grasp of the characteristics, expectations, and needs of their audience, as highlighted by Chen and Guan (2022). It also involves adapting their message to ensure the audience's comprehension, evoke empathy among them, and engage or entertain them. During the interviews, most participants mentioned their efforts to ensure that their works were understandable to their target audience. For instance, Jingjing explained her approach of making their works comprehensible to the audience. She mentioned providing both Chinese and English captions and adjusting their size appropriately to facilitate audience understanding. She also emphasized maintaining a pace that was neither too fast nor too slow. This aligns with the findings from the analysis of her group's work, which demonstrated the provision of both Chinese and English captions and a suitable pace, contributing to the audience's ease of comprehending the content (see Figure 2.6).

Figure 2.6 The bilingual captions in Jingjing's group work.

26 DMC competence conceptualization

Three participants highlighted their groups' endeavours to evoke empathy among the audience. Wang, for instance, mentioned that his group consistently used "you" throughout their composition to create a sense of shared experience with the audience. This approach aimed to make the audience feel they were in the same situation. Wang's comments about his peers' group work on family love also revealed that the selected background music, that is, "Hello, Tomorrow", was chosen to trigger feelings of homesickness among the audience.

In addition, three participants illustrated that their groups incorporated humour into their works to entertain the audience. Rainbow, for example, explained that her group consciously designed their work to be amusing, with the intention of capturing the audience's attention. She emphasized the importance of avoiding a tedious video, stating that humour was used to engage their classmates. For instance, they invited a flower-planting woman from their campus to participate in the project, and they chose the name "Alice" for the male character in the video, adding a playful touch to the narrative. These observations were consistent with the sample analysis, which indicated that Rainbow's group made deliberate efforts to entertain the audience. For instance, a humorous effect was created when Alice, after failing the college entrance exam, engaged in flower planting to earn money. In one scene, he was reprimanded by a seemingly stern flower-planting worker with humorous mispronunciations. The addition of bloopers at the end of the work further contributed to the entertainment effect (see Figure 2.7 for reference).

The L2 learners' *audience awareness* in the DMC project was in line with studies by Liaw and Accurso (2021), incorporating visual

  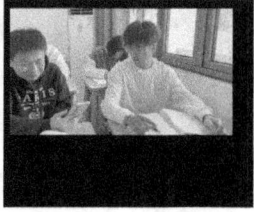

Figure 2.7 Alice, the flower-planting woman, and bloopers.

DMC competence conceptualization 27

pointers into videos to guide audience understanding, and Yeh (2018), emphasizing clear narration for audience comprehension. In addition, the use of the second-person singular pronoun to elicit empathy from the audience corresponded to Hafner's (2014) approach of interacting with the audience through such pronouns, and Bunch and Willett (2013) in which sympathy for the audience was evoked by presuming the audience's self-interests. Furthermore, the incorporation of humorous elements to capture the audience's attention and entertain them resonated with Hafner's (2014) findings, where students playfully adopted roles and included bloopers to add humour to their works.

Creativity

Creativity involves the generation of fresh materials to introduce various modes or the act of representing, recontextualizing, or transforming existing modes to create new meaning, as defined by the New London Group (1996). During the interviews, four participants shared that they engaged in creative processes to introduce multiple modes into their DMC projects. For instance, Sisi's group explained their approach of using original painting and paper-cutting techniques to depict a time-travel narrative involving an encounter between an ancient individual and a modern one. This creative approach was confirmed by the presence of the painting and paper-cutting elements in the sample analysis (see Figure 2.8). Moreover, observations made during Sisi's self-assessment in the classroom underscored their uniqueness in using these creative elements to illustrate the story.

Figure 2.8 The painting and paper cutting in Sisi's group work.

28 DMC competence conceptualization

Figure 2.9 The self-painting in Anastasia's group.

In a similar fashion, Anastasia mentioned that her group incorporated creativity into their project by designing animations and integrating their own original artwork, aiming to make their work stand out from others'. This creative effort was substantiated by the presence of the paintings in the sample analysis (see Figure 2.9). Anastasia's comments on other students' works further highlighted her appreciation of the inclusion of hand-drawn cartoon characters, acknowledging the creative elements in their projects.

Two participants articulated that rather than creating entirely new materials for modes, their groups opted to recontextualize and transform existing modes to convey new meaning. For instance, Cheng's group engaged in the recontextualization and transformation of video from television programmes to tell a story about deceptive tourism practices, drawing from their first-hand investigation. During the interviews, they explained that designing a TV programme from scratch was a challenging task, so they decided to repurpose a China Central Television (CCTV) news programme to integrate into their

DMC competence conceptualization 29

Figure 2.10 Cheng's group work on dishonesty.

narrative. This approach was supported by the sample analysis, which revealed the replacement of the images of two hosts with their own (see Figure 2.10 for reference).

Creativity was a prominent aspect of the L2 learners' DMC projects, evident in the innovative ways they designed their works. Notably, they crafted their narratives, echoing the findings in Oskoz and Elola (2016). Furthermore, the students displayed *creativity* by generating their own visual elements, such as paintings, paper cuts, and self-designed animations, to incorporate various modes into their compositions. This practice was consistent with observations made by King (2021) and Park (2021), which highlighted instances where students creatively produced their own visual content. In addition to creating their own modes, some students engaged in the recontextualization of existing modes, as demonstrated through the incorporation of content from the CCTV news programme to convey messages related to dishonesty. This showcased that *creativity* extends beyond the act of generating entirely new modes; it also encompasses the ability to repurpose, recontextualize, and transform available modes to construct new meaning, as emphasized by the New London Group (1996).

30 DMC competence conceptualization

Digital skills

Digital skills refers to proficiency in creating and editing videos. Classroom observations revealed that many L2 learners paid close attention to the digital aspects of their projects, specifically focusing on the sophistication and smoothness of the videos, as well as the effort invested in video creation and editing. For instance, Jack remarked on their own project, describing it as visually impressive and fancy. Hang, on the other hand, described their video as simple, comparing it to a PowerPoint presentation. Hao and Sun mentioned that their group members dedicated themselves to acquiring digital skills, particularly to ensuring the seamless integration of different modes and removing logos from videos downloaded from the internet. During the interviews, Anastasia acknowledged the significant contribution of Yuye in video editing and dubbing. This acknowledgment was consistent with the high-quality video displayed in their group project. The sample analysis further supported the notion that the majority of L2 learners demonstrated impressive digital skills in effectively presenting various modes, appropriately incorporating captions and dubbing, seamlessly combining modes, and incorporating special effects to entertain the audience.

Digital skills emerged as a distinctive aspect of DMC competence, marking a notable contribution to the study's findings. This finding resonated with the work of Jiang and Ren (2020), which underscored the importance of *digital skills* among L2 students and noted that the majority of these students expressed a desire for more comprehensive instruction in the digital aspects of DMC within the classroom. The absence of significant attention to *digital skills* in earlier studies pertaining to DMC competence may be attributed to educators' concerns that an excessive focus on *digital skills* could potentially divert learners from their primary goal of systematic English language acquisition.

Delivery

Delivery in this context pertains to how the DMC works are presented, encompassing elements such as rhythm, stress, pace, pitch, intonation, and tone within the videos. The focus group interviews indicated that the majority of students paid significant attention to this aspect when designing their DMC projects. Anastasia, for instance, shared that her

DMC competence conceptualization 31

group strove to adjust the pace of their work to ensure it matched their voiceover. Rainbow mentioned that they encountered challenges in synchronizing images and captions, requiring diligent efforts during the video editing process.

During classroom observations, most students provided comments and feedback that revolved around the delivery of their own and their peers' L2 DMC projects. They emphasized the importance of smooth and fluent presentation without interruptions. Some students pointed out specific issues they noticed in their peers' works, such as a three-second pause with a black screen, or variations in dubbing volume among group members.

Clarity, intelligibility, and pronunciation at an appropriate pace were also focal points. Students expressed concerns when dubbing was too fast or inconsistent in pace. They appreciated well-pronounced and clearly articulated dubbing, with attention to intonation patterns.

Furthermore, students addressed the works' captions in terms of their format, size, language, colour, font, and layout. Clear and legible captions were essential, as inadequate captions could hinder understanding. Feedback included comments on the absence of captions, capitalized texts, small-sized captions that lacked clarity, the importance of consistent colour and font choices, and the need to avoid overcrowding the screen with excessive texts. These observations highlighted the significance of effective *delivery* in creating engaging and comprehensible DMC works.

The *delivery* of DMC works emerged as a distinctive aspect of DMC competence, in line with previous research findings: Liang (2019) highlighted deliberate changes in pacing to enhance vocal emphasis; Yeh (2018) emphasized the importance of clear narration; and Liaw and Accurso (2021) stressed the significance of appropriate dubbing speed, rhythm, tonal variations, intonation, and well-placed pauses. The attention given to delivering works was closely linked to *audience awareness*, as these considerations aim to ensure that the audience comprehends and remains engaged with the content. In addition, *delivery* skills are intertwined with *digital skills*, as the adjustment of captions and dubbing relies on proficiency in video editing.

Cohesion of modes

Cohesion of modes in this context refers to the meaningful integration of various modes in ways that occur simultaneously, complement

32 *DMC competence conceptualization*

Figure 2.11 The concurrent relationship of modes in Siqi's group work.

each other, or diverge to effectively convey the topics addressed in the works, in accordance with Kress (2010). During the interviews, seven students disclosed that they employed modes concurrently to enhance the depth of their messaging. For instance, the interviews highlighted Siqi's group's approach, where they initially crafted the script and then sought relevant modes to reinforce their ideas. This methodology aligned with the findings from the sample analysis, which revealed this group's use of pictures, videos, and texts concurrently to convey the concept of luxurious consumption (see Figure 2.11).

This observation was consistent with the sample analysis, which showed the group's use of pictures and texts in a complementary manner. In this context, the pictures (i.e., drugs) and the accompanying texts ("he was increasingly greedy") conveyed different meanings but worked together to illustrate the negative consequences of being excessively obsessed with money (see Figure 2.12).

Only two participants mentioned that their groups intentionally employed divergent modes to create a humorous effect. In her interview, Rainbow explained that her group deliberately incorporated humorous music to contrast with Alice's unfortunate situation. This strategy involved a contradiction between the auditory and visual modes, which was intended to evoke humour. This approach was consistent with the findings from the sample analysis, where the divergence between Alice's misfortunes and the lively background music was evident.

DMC competence conceptualization 33

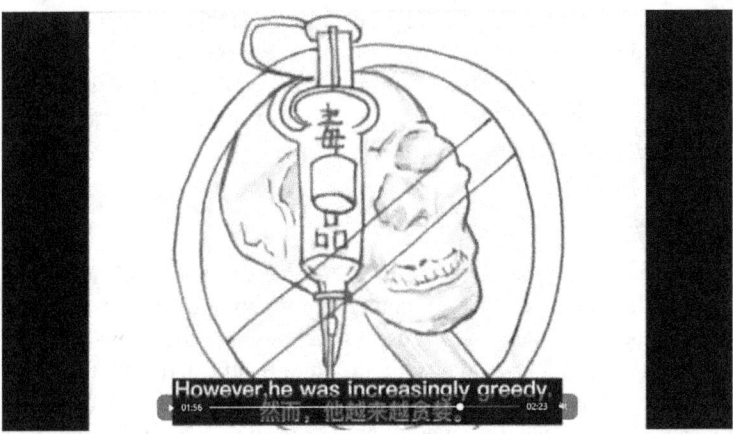

Figure 2.12 The complementary relationship of modes in Siqi's group work.

Additionally, during the interview, Rainbow highlighted the humorous element of using the name "Alice" for a male character in the story. By deviating from the conventional gender association of the name, the group aimed to add humour to their narrative and create the impression that the character might have a girlish disposition. This divergence in naming conventions further contributed to the humorous effect and the audience's perception of the character.

Cohesion of modes emerged as a noteworthy feature in the DMC works of L2 students. They effectively combined multiple modes in their compositions. This finding corroborated Hafner's (2014) research, where students integrated verbal and visual modes concurrently to convey the concept that appearances can be deceiving, particularly due to perceptual limitations. Moreover, the students complementarily combined modes by pairing visual elements with verbal components to immerse the audience in the scenes depicted. This observation meshed well with Hafner's (2014) findings, which noted the complementary use of modes to engage the audience more fully. The integration of modes further echoed Cimasko and Shin (2017), which highlighted how gestures complemented linguistic modes to emphasize personal emotions, and Park (2021), in which video clips and photos were used to complement lyrics and songs. Furthermore, the students creatively employed modes in a divergent manner to generate humorous effects within their works. This approach was consistent with Hafner's (2014) work, where divergence between seemingly mundane activities and lively audio elements created humour. The strategic divergence of modes to elicit specific effects highlights the creative capacities of the students, emphasizing their ability to employ multimodal composition for humour and engagement.

Identity expression

Identity expression pertains to how L2 learners reshape their identities through their created works, whether by reflecting on, reconstructing, or renegotiating their identities, as defined by the New London Group (1996). Most students in the study indicated that they primarily showcased their authentic identities. During the focus group interviews, Anastasia articulated that her group's work reflected their genuine identity as college students who lead digitally convenient lives. Similarly, Rainbow's and Sunny's groups expressed their intent to portray their authentic identities as college students striving to realize their dreams.

However, two groups chose to construct desirable identities through their works. Wen's group explored the identity of people who sought enjoyment in the virtual realm during the COVID-19 pandemic. They deliberately adopted this identity in their project, illustrating how people found entertainment in computer games. This not only reflected people's recreational activities during the pandemic but also conveyed their yearning to eliminate the virus and regain the freedom to engage in outdoor activities and face-to-face interactions. This portrayal was supported by the sample analysis, which featured a character in a game enjoying a visit to a valley and engaging in face-to-face communication with various creatures (see Figure 2.13).

Cheng's group explained that they aimed to conduct an investigation exposing the dishonest actions of internet influencers. To achieve this, they adopted the roles of TV hosts and reporters in their project to appear authoritative and persuasive. This assertion was confirmed by the sample analysis, which showed their construction of the roles of hosts and reporters within their project.

Identity expression was identified as another distinctive feature of DMC competence, echoing findings from previous studies, which showcased instances where students authentically portrayed their

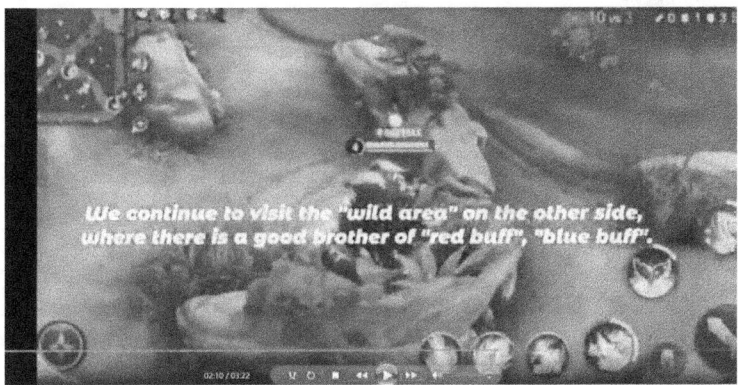

Figure 2.13 Wen's group work about a game character's travel.

real identities, such as individuals with significant social and political standing (Jiang & Gao, 2020), Congolese immigrants (Dávila & Susberry, 2021), or individuals characterized as Chinese writers, critical thinkers, meaning designers, oral narrators, and L2 writers (Liaw & Accurso, 2021). Moreover, they have featured students who demonstrated competence in L2 writing (Jiang, 2018), or who presented themselves as positive Tibetans, multimodal composers, multilingual speakers (Jiang et al., 2020), and bilingual, bicultural individuals (Smith et al., 2021). While many students portrayed their genuine identities, a few groups opted to construct alternative identities that diverged from their actual selves. This practice linked to instances where students assumed identities such as confident students with native-like English proficiency, despite the reality suggesting otherwise (Cimasko & Shin, 2017). Additionally, this was compatible with situations where students adopted roles such as "expert scientist", "reporter", or "traveller" to convey specific narratives or themes, as seen in Hafner's (2014) work. The *expression of identity* in DMC projects is closely tied to *creativity*, as students' creative endeavours, whether in designing new materials or appropriating existing modes, contribute to the construction of unique and desirable identities. What is more, *identity expression* is linked to *genre awareness*, as students may assume various roles and present different identities depending on the specific genre they are working within.

Language use

Language use in this context refers to the accurate and appropriate use of language in captions and dubbing within the DMC projects. The participants unanimously emphasized the significance of linguistic accuracy. In the focus group interviews, Yuye mentioned her role in dubbing and emphasized the importance of practising the script multiple times to ensure accurate pronunciation. This dedication to pronunciation accuracy was corroborated by the sample analysis, which indicated precise pronunciation in her group's work. Angel also mentioned in the interview that their group revised the script multiple times before incorporating it into the video, aligning with the sample analysis that reflected the presence of accurate scripts.

Moreover, the majority of participants stressed their attention to *linguistic choices* suited to different genres. As previously discussed in the section on *genre awareness*, students reported adapting their language to match the specific genre of their project. For instance, Sisi's group used oral and humorous language in the form of dialogue, frequently incorporating emotional words appropriate to the narrative genre. Siqi's group opted for more formal and perspective-taking language suitable for the argumentation genre, while Anastasia's group utilized formal and objective language suited to the exposition genre. Additionally, participants revealed that they manipulated linguistic choices to evoke empathy among the audience. For example, Wang incorporated second-person singular pronouns in his work to establish a sense of interaction with the audience, intending to foster empathy.

Accurate and appropriate *language use* was identified as a crucial element of DMC competence, reinforcing the significance of this aspect in evaluating L2 learners' DMC performance. This observation was consistent with the findings of Hafner and Ho (2020), Kim et al. (2022), and Elola and Oskoz (2022), which highlighted teachers' emphasis on the accuracy of pronunciation, vocabulary, and grammar in the assessment of L2 learners' DMC work. It is worth noting that this discovery may alleviate concerns among educators that DMC might detract from linguistic learning, as students demonstrated a commitment to language proficiency in addition to their engagement with non-linguistic modes. Plus, the effective *use of language* is closely intertwined with *genre awareness*, as different genres necessitate specific linguistic styles and choices. Additionally, *language use* is directly related to *audience awareness*, as learners make conscious linguistic choices to evoke empathy or entertain their audience.

Organization

Organization pertains to how the DMC works were structured or organized. The majority of participants reported that they employed various organizational structures in their DMC projects. According to the interviews, Sisi's and Sunny's groups organized their digital stories chronologically, presenting events in the order in which they occurred. Chang's group used a cause-effect structure, initially illustrating the development of digital technology and subsequently highlighting its impact on people's lives. Xinyi's and Jingjing's groups followed a problem-solution pattern. For example, Xinyi's group first identified the problem of young people spending limited time with their parents due to work commitments and then proposed solutions to address this issue, such as promoting a healthy parent-child relationship and advising parents to be more independent. Similarly, Jingjing's group outlined the problem of young people lacking face-to-face communication and suggested solutions like turning off mobile phones and socializing with friends. These findings were consistent with the sample analyses of the respective groups, confirming the employment of their chosen organizational structures.

Organization emerged as a vital component of DMC competence. L2 learners displayed organizational skills by structuring their works according to the typical patterns of introduction, main body, and conclusion. This structure dovetailed with the opening-body-ending structure observed in Hafner's (2014) work. In some instances, learners followed a statement-subpoints-conclusion thesis pattern, partially resembling the statement-five-paragraph thesis structure described in Bunch and Willett (2013). In expositional video essays, students employed cause-effect and problem-solution structures, while narratives were organized chronologically. This focus on *organization*, particularly within the context of narration, is an area that has received relatively little attention in previous studies. Notably, no samples discussed in this chapter adhered to academic writing genres, such as the introduction-method-result-discussion structure seen in Tardy (2005), or the 5R text structure featured in Smith et al. (2021). It is important to highlight the connection between *organization* and *genre awareness*, as different genres necessitate distinct organizational approaches.

On the basis of the L2 student DMC competence model discussed earlier in this chapter, Chapter 3 proceeds to develop a scale for assessing L2 student DMC competence, and Chapter 4 assembles validity evidence for interpretation and use of this L2 student DMC competence scale. Chapter 5 goes further by applying the scale in L2 classrooms to guide students' self- and peer-assessment practices in the DMC project.

Implications of this model

It is important to acknowledge that further analysis of additional genres may be necessary, and this model may require revisions to accommodate different DMC genres. DMC competence is a multifaceted concept, and this model represents an initial attempt to move beyond the elusive conceptualization of DMC competence. Future studies can explore more genres and refine this model accordingly.

The model has important implications for both the teaching of and research into DMC and L2 writing. It furnishes theoretical foundations for DMC competence, offering valuable guidance for measuring, instructing, and assessing this competence. Future research endeavours can operationalize and develop tools to gauge DMC competence and track its development over time. It is noteworthy that the research in this chapter was conducted within a specific L2 context, involving participants with low to intermediate English proficiency, so the generalizability of the findings to other contexts might be limited. Subsequent studies could analyze samples from more advanced students in various instructional settings for writing.

Furthermore, considering that DMC competence has not yet been widely incorporated into L2 curricula and syllabi, the model proposed in this chapter could be of interest to curriculum designers and educational policymakers. It might encourage the integration of DMC competence into L2 curricula, offering guidance on what to teach students to excel in DMC projects, how to design relevant classroom activities that nurture DMC competence, and how to implement more effective formative assessments to provide constructive feedback to students. Additionally, this model could aid in the development of appropriate and meaningful assessment scales for evaluating students' DMC performance.

Lastly, this research can empower L2 learners by providing them with a clear understanding of DMC competence. This understanding might motivate students to self-assess their DMC competence, set personal goals, monitor their progress in developing this competence, reflect on their strengths and areas needing improvement, and ultimately become proficient DMC designers.

Summary of this chapter

This chapter has explored L2 student DMC competence by drawing on related theories, previous empirical studies, and the data obtained through student focus group interviews, classroom observations, and sample analysis. We discovered that L2 student DMC competence is a multi-dimensional concept encompassing nine key dimensions: *utilization of multiple modes, genre awareness* (including the subcategory of *audience awareness*), *digital skills, creativity, delivery, cohesion, identity expression, language use* (which includes the subcategory of *linguistic choices*), and *organization*.

Questions for further discussion

Please think about the following questions based on what you have just learnt about the L2 student DMC competence model.

For teachers:

1. How does the L2 student DMC competence model differ from print-based monomodal writing competence? How do these discrepancies impede the implementation of the DMC project in my context?
2. What are the possible barriers if I am about to incorporate DMC competence into the English writing curriculum? How am I going to overcome these barriers?
3. What are my students' current levels of DMC competence? How am I going to arrange learning activities or provide instructional interventions for them to develop their competence?
4. Which aspects of L2 DMC competence do my students excel at? Which aspects do they struggle with?
5. How does this model inform my assessment of DMC or other technology-enhanced L2 writing tasks?

For researchers:

1. What are the relationships among the components of L2 student DMC competence?
2. How does this model differ from other standards of language competence among learners, such as the Common European Framework of Reference for Languages (CEFR) and China's Standards of English (CSE)?
3. How can the L2 student DMC competence model be revised to accommodate different DMC genres?
4. How can this model inform research that measures L2 student DMC competence and the relationships between it and other relevant variables, such as motivation, self-regulation, and L2 proficiency?

References

Barthes, R. (1977). *Image–Music–Text*. Fontana Press.

Barton, D., & Hamilton, M. (1998). *Local literacies: Reading and writing in one community*. Routledge.

Bateman, J. A. (2014). *Text and image: A critical introduction to the visual/verbal divide*. Routledge.

Bunch, G. C., & Willett, K. (2013). Writing to mean in middle school: Understanding how second language writers negotiate textually-rich content-area instruction. *Journal of Second Language Writing, 22*, 141–160.

Chen, Y., & Guan, X. Y. (2022). To whom do I write? Chinese EFL test-takers' conceptualization and construction of their audience in the Aptis writing test. In J. Yan. & L. Hamp-Lyons (Eds.), *Assessing the English language writing of Chinese learners of English* (pp. 49–70). Springer.

Cimasko, T., & Shin, D. (2017). Multimodal resemiotization and authorial agency in an L2 writing classroom. *Written Communication, 34*(4), 387–413.

Dávila, L. T., & Susberry, V. (2021). Multimodal and multilingual co-authoring in high school social studies ESL classrooms. In D. Shin, T. Cimasko, & Y. Yi (Eds.), *Multimodal composing in K-16 ESL and EFL education: Multilingual perspectives* (pp. 55–71). Springer.

Denzin, N. K. (1970). *The research act: A theoretical introduction to sociological methods*. Aldine.

Eisner, E. W. (1991). *The enlightened eye: Qualitative inquiry and the enhancement of educational practice*. Collier Macmillan Canada.

Elola, I., & Oskoz, A. (2022). Reexamining feedback on L2 digital writing. *Studies in Second Language Learning and Teaching, 12*(4), 575–595.

Fairclough, N. (1995). *Critical discourse analysis: A critical study of language*. Longman.

Gee, J. P. (2005). *An introduction to discourse analysis: Theory and method* (2nd ed.). Routledge.

Hafner, C. A. (2014). Embedding digital literacies in English language teaching: Students' digital video projects as multimodal ensembles. *TESOL Quarterly, 48*, 655–685.

Hafner, C. A., & Ho, W. Y. J. (2020). Assessing digital multimodal composing in second language writing: Towards a process-based model. *Journal of Second Language Writing, 47*, 100710.

Hava, K. (2021). Exploring the role of digital storytelling in student motivation and satisfaction in EFL education. *Computer Assisted Language Learning, 34*(7), 958–978.

Jiang, L. (2017). The affordances of digital multimodal composing for EFL learning. *ELT Journal, 71*(4), 413–422.

Jiang, L. (2018). Digital multimodal composing and investment change in learners' writing in English as a foreign language. *Journal of Second Language Writing, 40*, 60–72.

Jiang, L., & Gao, J. (2020). Fostering EFL learners' digital empathy through multimodal composing. *RELC Journal, 51*(1), 70–85.

Jiang, L. & Ren, W. (2020). Digital multimodal composing in L2 learning: Ideologies and impact. *Journal of Language, Identity & Education, 20*(3), 167–182.

Jiang, L., Yang, M., & Yu, S. (2020). Chinese ethnic minority students' investment in English learning empowered by digital multimodal composing. *TESOL Quarterly, 54*(4), 954–979.

Jiang, L., Yu, S., & Lee, I. (2022). Developing a genre-based model for assessing digital multimodal composing in second language writing: Integrating theory with practice. *Journal of Second Language Writing, 57*, 100869.

Jiang, L., Yu, S., & Zhao, Y. (2019). Teacher engagement with digital multimodal composing in a Chinese tertiary EFL curriculum. *Language Teaching Research, 25*(4), 613–632.

Jick, T. D. (1979). Mixing qualitative and quantitative methods: Triangulation in action. *Administrative Science Quarterly, 24*, 602–611.

Jones, R. H., & Hafner, C. A. (2012). *Understanding digital literacies: A practical introduction*. Routledge.

Kim, Y., Kang, S., Nam, Y., & Skalicky, S. (2022). Peer interaction, writing proficiency, and the quality of collaborative digital multimodal composing task: Comparing guided and unguided planning. *System, 106*(4), 102722.

King, N. (2021). Designing a better place: Multimodal multilingual composition. In D. Shin, T. Cimasko, & Y. Yi (Eds.), *Multimodal composing in K-16 ESL and EFL education: Multilingual perspectives* (pp. 147–162). Springer.

Kloepfer, R. (1977). Komplementarität von Sprache und Bild. Am Beispiel von Comic, Karikatur und Reklame. In R. Posner & H. P. Reinecke (Eds.), *Zeichenprozesse. Semiotische Forschung in den Einzelwissenschaften* (pp. 129–145). Athenäum.

Kress, G. (2000). Multimodality: Challenges to thinking about language. *TESOL Quarterly, 34*(2), 337–340.

Kress, G. (2003). *Literacy in the new media age*. Routledge.

Kress, G. (2010). *Multimodality: A social semiotic approach to contemporary communication*. Routledge.

Kress, G. (2017). What is a mode?. In C. Jewitt (Ed.), *The Routledge handbook of multimodal analysis* (pp. 54–67). Routledge.

Lee, S.-Y., Lo, Y.-H., & Chin, T.-C. (2019). Practicing multiliteracies to enhance EFL learners' meaning making process and language development: A multimodal problem-based approach. *Computer Assisted Language Learning, 34*(1–2), 66–91.

Liang, M-Y. (2019). Beyond elocution: Multimodal narrative discourse analysis of L2 storytelling. *ReCALL, 31*(1), 56–74.

Liaw, M. J., & Accurso, K. (2021). Design and opportunity in critical multilingual/multimodal composing pedagogy. In D. Shin, T. Cimasko, & Y. Yi (Eds.), *Multimodal composing in K-16 ESL and EFL education: Multilingual perspectives* (pp.89–108). Springer.

Mackey, A., & Gass, S. M. (2005). *Second language research: Methodology and design*. Lawrence Erlbaum.

McKee, H. A., & DeVoss, D. N. (Eds.). (2013). *Digital writing assessment & evaluation*. Computers and Composition Digital Press/Utah State University Press.

Nelson, M. E. (2006). Mode, meaning, and synaesthesia in multimedia L2 writing. *Language, Learning, & Technology, 19*(2), 56–76.

New London Group. (1996). A pedagogy of multiliteracies: Designing social futures. *Harvard Educational Review, 66*(1), 60–92.

O'Halloran, K., & Smith, B. (2013). Multimodality and technology. In C. Chapelle. (Ed), *Encyclopedia of Applied Linguistics* (pp. 1–5). Wiley-Blackwell.

Oskoz, A., & Elola, I. (2016). Digital stories: Bringing multimodal texts to the Spanish writing classroom. *ReCALL, 28*(3), 326–342.

Park, J. H. (2021). "Dear future me": Connecting college L2 writers' literacy paths to an envisioned future self through a multimodal project. In D. Shin, T. Cimasko, & Y. Yi (Eds.), *Multimodal composing in K-16 ESL and EFL education: Multilingual perspectives* (pp. 73–86). Springer.

Shin, D., & Cimasko, T. (2008). Multimodal composition in a college ESL class: New tools, traditional norms. *Computers and Composition, 25*(4), 376–395.

Smith, B. E., Malova, I., & Amgott, N. (2021). Expanding meaning-making possibilities: Bilingual students' perspectives on multimodal composing. In D. Shin, T. Cimasko, & Y. Yi (Eds.), *Multimodal composing in K-16 ESL and EFL education: Multilingual perspectives* (pp.109–124). Springer.

Tardy, C. (2005). Expressions of disciplinarity and individuality in a multimodal genre. *Computers and Composition, 22*(3), 319–336.

Unsworth, L. (2008). Multiliteracies and metalanguage: Describing image/text relations as a resource for negotiating multimodal texts. In J. Coiro, M. Knobel, C. Lankshear, & D. J. Leu (Eds.), *Handbook of research on new literacies* (pp. 377–405). Erlbaum.

Wang, H. (2008). *A case study of English language learners' multimodal compositions and identity representations compositions and identity representations* [Unpublished doctoral dissertation]. Georgia State University.

Yeh, H-C. (2018). Exploring the perceived benefits of the process of multimodal video making in developing multiliteracies. *Language Learning & Technology, 22*(2), 28–37.

Yi, Y., & Hirvela, A. (2010). Technology and 'self-sponsored' writing: A case study of a young Korean American. *Computers and Composition, 27*(2), 94–111.

Yi, Y., King, N., & Safriani, A. (2017). Reconceptualizing assessment for digital multimodal literacy. *TESOL Journal, 8*(4), 878–885.

Yin, R. K. (2016). *Qualitative research from start to finish* (2nd ed.). The Guilford Press.

Zhang, E. D., & Yu, S. (2023b). Conceptualizing digital multimodal composing competence in L2 classroom: A qualitative inquiry. *Computer Assisted Language Learning*. Advance online publication.

Zheng, S. (2017a). *New horizon College English 1 reading & writing* (3rd ed.). Shanghai Jiao Tong University Press.

Zheng, S. (2017b). *New horizon College English 1 listening & speaking* (3rd ed.). Shanghai Jiao Tong University Press.

Appendix

Student Focus Group Interview Protocol

Date	
Time	
Interviewer	
Interviewee	
Icebreaking question	Do you like the project?
Interview questions	1. Did you use multiple modes in your work? Mode refers to the resources you used such as pictures, audios, videos, role-plays, animations, sound effects, and the like. 2. What genre did you adopt in your work? Why did you choose this genre? What are the features of your work (e.g., the linguistic style, the use of words, the tone, the organization of your work)? 3. Did you consider audience in designing your work? How did you meet the audience's needs? 4. Do you think that you showed creativity in your work? In which way did you demonstrate your creativity? 5. Did you pay attention to the delivery of your work such as the size, form, color, layout of captions, the intelligibility of the dubbing or the pace, rhyme, tone, intonation and so forth? 6. How did you combine the modes you collected or created? Did you concurrently, complementarily or divergently combine the modes? 7. Did you intend to show any identity through your work? What kind of identity it is? 8. Did you attend to language such as the accuracy and appropriacy in the captions and dubbing in your DMC works? 9. How did you organize your work? Does it follow any structures? 10. Did you use any other skills in making the L2 DMC works? What are those skills? How did you use those skills?
Concluding statement	Thank you for your time! Do you have any questions about the interview?

3 Scale development for assessing L2 student digital multimodal composing competence

Introduction

While Chapter 2 provides an L2 student DMC competence model, few instruments have been specifically constructed to measure student DMC competence in the L2 context. Launching DMC projects without assessing L2 students' competence may have negative consequences. For instance, without clarifying the learning goals of DMC, L2 students tend to be disoriented and might devote time and energy to honing skills that are irrelevant in creating their DMC artifacts. They may also lack the motivation to participate in the DMC projects and regard DMC competence as an optional add-on (Mills & Exley, 2014). Teachers are likely to struggle to evaluate the effectiveness of their DMC intervention as an instructional approach. Therefore, there is a pressing need to develop an L2 student DMC competence scale to evaluate L2 students' DMC competence and the learning evidence from participating in DMC projects.

Based on the L2 student DMC competence model proposed in Chapter 2, this chapter aims to delineate the process of developing just such an L2 student DMC competence scale, inclusive of defining the construct, drafting the items, and analyzing the items via exploratory factor analysis (EFA).

Developing an L2 student DMC competence scale

The development of the L2 student DMC competence scale includes defining the construct, constructing items, and analyzing items. The procedures are presented in Figure 3.1.

DOI: 10.4324/9781003475729-3

46 DMC competence scale development

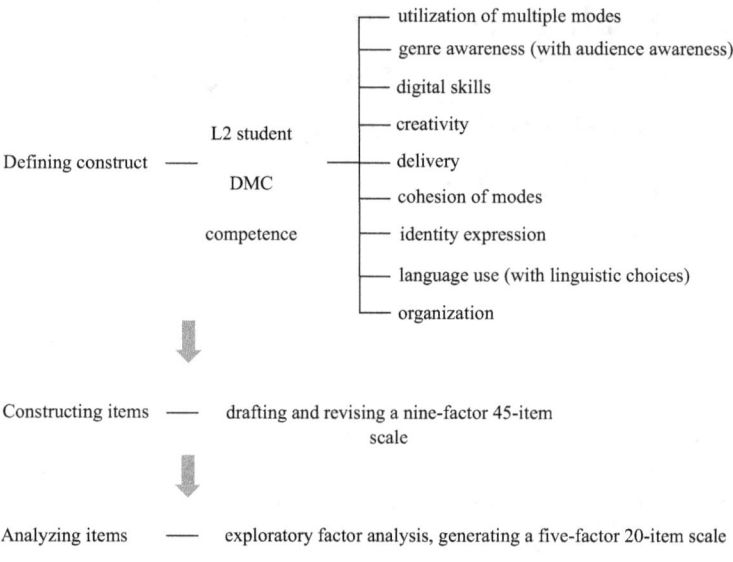

Figure 3.1 The processes of developing the L2 student DMC competence scale.

Defining the construct

Drawing on the L2 student DMC competence model proposed in Chapter 2, the construct for L2 student DMC competence encompasses *utilization of multiple modes, genre awareness* (with the subcategory of *audience awareness*), *digital skills, creativity, delivery, cohesion of modes, identity expression, language use* (with the subcategory of *linguistic choices*), and *organization*. As this model was informed by the DMC competence literature and based on L2 student DMC designers' perceptions of the DMC competence utilized in creating DMC works, it contains rich features of DMC competence:

- *Utilization of multiple modes*: Deployment of numerous modes in DMC projects, such as texts, images, colour, layout, videos, music, sounds, animation, and role-plays.
- *Genre awareness*: Conscious manipulation of language and organizational structures for different genres to serve intended purposes

and audiences, and understanding of the audience's features, expectations, and needs.
- *Creativity*: Creating new materials to introduce modes, or representing, recontextualizing, or transforming available modes to convey new meanings.
- *Digital skills*: Making and editing videos.
- *Delivery*: Presentation of the DMC works, including rhythm, stress, pace, pitch, intonation, and tone of the videos.
- *Cohesion of modes*: Meaningful combination of modes in concurrent, complementary, and divergent manners to deliver the messages of the works.
- *Identity expression*: L2 learners remaking themselves through the works designed by reflecting on, reconstructing, or renegotiating their identities.
- *Language use*: Accurate and appropriate use of language in captions and dubbing, and appropriate *linguistic choices* for specific genres and audiences.
- *Organization*: How the DMC works were organized or structured in this study.

Constructing items

Based on the L2 student DMC competence model, items were also brainstormed based on the definitions of each dimension. Adhering to the guidelines of scale development (Dörnyei, 2003), at least four items were drafted for each L2 student DMC competence dimension (DeVellis, 2017; Dörnyei, 2003; Dörnyei, & Taguchi, 2010). Items were rejected if they were lengthy, ambiguous, or captured multiple ideas. All items were positively worded, and deployed a 5-point Likert response scale: Ratings of 1, 2, 3, 4, and 5 corresponded to strongly disagree, disagree, neutral, agree, and strongly agree, respectively.

After that, the scale was translated into Mandarin Chinese, and three Ph.D. students reviewed the translation of the items and provided suggestions about some inaccurate areas. Three experts in the field of DMC and L2 writing were consulted to elicit their suggestions for the scale. One expert noted that the item *I do not imitate others' L2 DMC work, and try to make my work original* was imprecise in that imitation is an indispensable part of the redesigning process. Therefore, this item was dropped. He also suggested adding examples of organization to the item *I follow a structure in writing the script of the L2 DMC work*, and it was therefore revised to *I can use organizations such as introduction-main body-conclusion, cause-effect, compare-contrast, problem-solution, and the like in writing the script of the L2 DMC work* to aid participants' comprehension of it. Another expert stated that several items in *creativity* were similar in terms of the meaning of giving references (e.g., *I can give credit to the authors or owners of the modes*; *I know that using the modes without giving references is plagiarism*; *I can provide the sources for all modes used in my L2 DMC work*; *I can pay attention to the sources of modes when I collect them*), and could be synthesized into one item. Hence, the single item *I can give references to the modes* was used to capture the important feature of *creativity*, i.e., giving credit for the available modes, in the DMC design process.

The scale was then distributed for pilot testing to 15 students who had participated in the student focus group interviews about DMC competence mentioned in Chapter 2. Most students acknowledged that the scale comprehensively captured the DMC competence utilized by them. This was exemplified by Anastasia and Lily's statements:

The scale provides a full picture of the abilities and skills used in the DMC project. (Anastasia)

The items are comprehensive, covering almost all the important aspects of the skills we used in designing DMC works. (Lily)

That said, they revealed that some expressions were difficult to comprehend. For instance, Wen stated that:

Some words are abstract and confusing to me, such as "建构意义" (make meaning) in the item 我知道多模态在建构意义方面的作用是强大的. *What does "建构" refer to? It appears kind of strange to me. In addition, "立人设" (construct identity) in the item* 我可以在多模态写作作品中"立人设" *is weird, as it has derogatory meanings. I am not sure whether it is relevant to the DMC project.*

The first author clarified the meanings that puzzled Wen and elicited her suggestions about revisions to address these issues. After discussion, we revised "建构意义" to "表达意义" to make it more approachable to students, and "立人设" to "展示形象" to avoid the negative connotation.

Snow mentioned that "*'幻想的身份' in the item 我可以在英语多模态写作的故事中展示一些幻想的身份 appears weird, as '幻想' means deviating a lot from the reality. I think that '想象' might be more accurate, which highlights the imagination based on the reality, as we tend to assume some common identities like TV hosts, tourist guides, reporters, and so forth.*"

The first author agreed with Snow; "想象" corresponds with "imagine", while "幻想" is more germanely translated as "fancy". After discussion, we reached a consensus and the item was revised to 我可以通过作品构建一个想象中的身份.

Some students observed that the scale was lengthy, as the original version contained 56 items (three were deleted after expert judgment). This was illustrated by Cheng:

There are so many items and reading the scale is sort of time-consuming. It is also exhausting to read the items one by one.

Considering the high cognitive load involved in reading a large number of items, we double-checked the scale items, removed some that had similar meanings, and reduced the total to 45 items.

The first version of the scale, which was a nine-factor 45-item scale, is presented in Table 3.1.

Analyzing items

EFA was conducted on the 250 participants' self-reported scores on the nine-factor 45-item L2 student DMC competence scale to examine the factorial structure of the scale. The assumptions of factor analysis were inspected. The Kaiser–Meyer–Olkin measure of sampling adequacy (KMO) was .933, close to 1, indicating that factor analysis can generate reliable and distinct factors. The value was meritorious based on Hutcheson and Sofroniou's criterion (1999). Bartlett's test of sphericity was significant ($x^2 (990) = 6081.109$, $p = .000$), indicating that the correlations between variables are significantly different from zero. To extract the most appropriate number of factors, we referred to Kaiser's (1960) criterion of using eigenvalues exceeding 1. We requested that all loadings less than 0.4 be suppressed (Field, 2009).

Table 3.1 The first version of the L2 student DMC competence scale

---

The L2 student DMC competence scale
5 strongly agree
4 agree
3 neutral
2 disagree
1 strongly disagree

Utilization of multiple modes
I can use multiple modes in my work.
I know that multiple modes are powerful in making meaning.
I can use multiple modes to enrich my work.
I can use multiple modes to support my argument.
I can vary the use of modes in my work.

Genre awareness
I can make my work comprehensible to the audience.
I can consider the audience's reading and listening comprehension abilities in my work.
I know that works of different genres have different features and styles.
I know that different audiences may prefer different modes.
I can choose apt modes according to the genres.
I can add humour to make my work entertaining to the audience.
I can arouse compassion among the audience to engage them.

Digital skills
I know how to edit videos.
I know how to insert captions.
I know how to shoot videos.
I know how to do dubbing for the work.
I know how to add special effects to my work.

Creativity
I can create modes such as drawing, animation, or role-play.
I can assign new meaning to the modes collected from the internet.
I can give references to the modes.
I can convey my creative ideas through DMC works.

Cohesion of modes
I can use modes that complement each other to "fill in gaps" in meaning.
I can use modes with similar meanings to reinforce each other.
I can use modes that relate to the topic of the work.
I can use modes with different meanings to create specific effects like humour or irony.
I can combine modes to achieve cohesion of the meaning.

Table 3.1 (Continued)

Delivery
I can pay attention to my manners and attitudes in the narration and role-play.
I can use appropriate rhythm and pace in my work.
I can use appropriate tone and intonation in the dubbing of the DMC work.
I can use appropriate stress and pauses in the dubbing of the DMC work.
I can use accurate and fluent pronunciation in my dubbing.

Language use
I can avoid grammatical mistakes in the DMC work.
I can use accurate vocabulary in the DMC work.
I can use complex and diverse words in my work.
I can use complex and diverse sentence structures in my work.

Organization
I can clearly present the organization of my work.
I can use different organizations according to the genres of my DMC work.
I can use organizations such as introduction-main body-conclusion, cause-effect, compare-contrast, problem-solution, and the like.
I can express my ideas logically in my work.

Identity expression
I can showcase my real individual identity through my work.
I can construct a desirable identity through my work which may contradict my real identity.
I can showcase the identity of a certain group through my work.
I can construct an imagined identity through the work.
I can take on certain roles in the work.
I know that DMC work needs to show the designers' identities.

EFA with maximum likelihood estimation and varimax rotation was conducted with SPSS Statistics 21.0 software.

The EFA analysis suggested a nine-factor solution. Item analysis showed that three factors lacked interpretability, so these were eliminated. Items which had low factor loadings were explored. Items with loadings less than 0.4 were dropped. The interpretability is the criterion to decide upon which factor(s) cross-loading items cluster. The outcome of this item-analysis process was the removal of 25 items, leaving a total of 20 items. Every item dropped was considered closely by the researchers, and it turned out that all the rejections had clear justifications due to low loadings, lack of interpretability, or similarity to other items. The final five-factor solution (i.e., factor 1 *digital skills*, factor 2 *creativity*, factor 3 *genre awareness*, factor 4 *language use*, and factor 5 *cohesion of modes*) explained 52.268% of the total variances of L2 student DMC competence. *Digital skills was* the strongest factor in explaining the variance of L2 DMC competence (36.628%). Other factors had similar explanatory power, and explained variances ranging from 3.005% to 4.809%. The factor loadings of all items are shown in Table 3.2. The final version of the scale is presented in Table 3.3.

Table 3.2 Factor loadings and variances of the 20-item L2 student DMC competence scale

Items	F1	F2	F3	F4	F5
I know how to edit videos.	.705				
I know how to shoot videos.	.687				
I know how to do dubbing for the work.	.541				
I know how to add special effects to my work.	.759				
I can create modes such as drawing, animation, or role-play.		.530			
I can assign new meaning to the modes collected from the internet.		.730			
I can give references to the modes.		.429			
I can use different organizations according to the genres of my DMC work.			.546		
I can use organizations such as introduction-main body-conclusion, cause-effect, compare-contrast, problem-solution, and the like.			.548		
I can make my work comprehensible to the audience.			.516		

Table 3.2 (Continued)

Items	F1	F2	F3	F4	F5
I know that works of different genres have different features and styles.			.446		
I can add humour to make my work entertaining to the audience.			.683		
I can use appropriate tone and intonation in the dubbing of the DMC work.				.589	
I can use appropriate stress and pauses in the dubbing of the DMC work.				.592	
I can avoid grammatical mistakes in the DMC work.				.613	
I can use accurate vocabulary in the DMC work.				.753	
I can use modes that relate to the topic of the work.					.725
I can combine modes to achieve cohesion of the meaning.					.423
I can use modes that complement each other to "fill in gaps" in meaning.					.731
I can use modes with similar meanings to reinforce each other.					.737

Table 3.3 The EFA-generated L2 student DMC competence scale

Digital skills
I know how to edit videos.
I know how to shoot videos.
I know how to do dubbing for the work.
I know how to add special effects to my work.

Creativity
I can create modes such as drawing, animation, or role-play.
I can assign new meaning to the modes collected from the internet.
I can give references to the modes.

Genre awareness
I can use different organizations according to the genres of my DMC work.
I can use organizations such as introduction-main body-conclusion, cause-effect, compare-contrast, problem-solution, and the like.
I can make my work comprehensible to the audience.
I know that works of different genres have different features and styles.
I can add humour to make my work entertaining to the audience.

Language use
I can use appropriate tone and intonation in the dubbing of the DMC work.
I can use appropriate stress and pauses in the dubbing of the DMC work.
I can avoid grammatical mistakes in the DMC work.
I can use accurate vocabulary in the DMC work.

Cohesion of modes
I can use modes that relate to the topic of the work.
I can combine modes to achieve cohesion of the meaning.
I can use modes that complement each other to "fill in gaps" in meaning.
I can use modes with similar meanings to reinforce each other.

Summary and implications of this chapter

Chapter 3 has outlined the process of creating an assessment scale for evaluating L2 student DMC competence. It has defined the construct of competence as a nine-dimensional construct, encompassing *utilization of multiple modes*, *genre awareness* (with the subcategory of *audience awareness*), *digital skills*, *creativity*, *delivery*, *cohesion*, *identity expression*, *language use* (with the subcategory of *linguistic choices*), and *organization*, discussed the item development process, and presented data collection and analysis. Through EFA analysis, the chapter has identified five distinct factors, i.e., *digital skills* with four

DMC competence scale development 55

items, *creativity* with three items, *genre awareness* with five items, *language use* with four items, and *cohesion of modes* with four items. This chapter serves as a pivotal step towards creating a valuable tool that comprehensively captures L2 student DMC competence for assessing the multifaceted abilities of L2 students in the DMC context. The scale specifies the learning goals of DMC projects and provides guidance for curriculum designers to incorporate DMC into curricula and syllabi. It is also useful to students in monitoring the progress of their own DMC projects based on their goals and self-evaluating the strengths and weaknesses of their DMC competence. Teachers can draw on the scale to evaluate students' DMC competence, obtain student learning evidence from DMC projects, and gauge the effectiveness of their DMC interventions.

Questions for further discussion

Study and discuss the following questions:

For teachers:

1. Are the five dimensions of the L2 student DMC competence scale, i.e., *digital skills, genre awareness, creativity, language use*, and *cohesion of modes*, relevant to the L2 curriculum in my context?
2. Which dimension of the L2 student DMC competence scale aligns with my teaching objectives in the L2 context? What class activities can I design to nurture skills relevant to this dimension?
3. What are the benefits of using the scale if I plan to set up a DMC project in my classroom?
4. How does using the scale facilitate assessment as learning practices in my classroom?

For students:

1. Do I need the L2 student DMC competence scale for my DMC project? How does this scale guide my design of DMC artifacts?
2. How might the scale guide my peer- and self-assessment practices?
3. Do I like scales or sample works to identify the success criteria for your DMC project?

References

DeVellis, R. F. (2017). *Scale development: Theory and applications* (4th ed.). Sage.
Dörnyei, Z. (2003). *Questionnaires in second language research*. Routledge.
Dörnyei, Z., & Taguchi, T. (2010). *Questionnaires in second language research: Construction, administration, and processing*. Routledge.
Field, A. P. (2009). *Discovering statistics using SPSS* (3rd ed.). Sage.
Hutcheson, G., & Sofroniou, N. (1999). *The multivariate social scientist*. Sage.
Kaiser, H. F. (1960). The application of electronic computers to factor analysis. *Educational and Psychological Measurement, 20*, 141–151.
Mills, K. A., & Exley, B. (2014). Time, space, and text in the elementary school digital writing classroom. *Written Communication, 31*(4), 434–469.

4 Scale validation for assessing L2 student digital multimodal composing competence

Introduction

Validation refers to marshalling evidence to demonstrate that "(the) test measures what it purports to measure" (Sireci, 2009, p. 28), and the extent to which both empirical evidence and theoretical justifications support the appropriateness and accuracy of interpreting and utilizing scores from assessments (Messick, 1989). After the L2 student DMC competence had been developed, as outlined in Chapter 3, construct validity evidence was assembled to justify the meaningfulness of the scores derived from the scale. This chapter depicts the validation process for the L2 student DMC competence scale.

The validation process for the L2 student DMC competence scale was guided by Messick's construct validity framework (1995). The concept of validity has been conventionally perceived as comprising three components, i.e., content validity, criterion-related validity, and construct validity (Anastasi, 1986; Angoff, 1988; Geisinger, 1992; Law & Baum, 2005; Yun & Ulrich, 2002). However, this tripartite perspective on validity has its shortcomings. Firstly, it can be challenging to distinguish between different types of validity, such as the subtle distinctions between concurrent validity and convergent validity. Secondly, the tripartite validity categories may give the misleading impression that validity is a fixed trait of a test, instrument, or scale, rather than a dynamic quality that evolves over time and through ongoing processes (Messick, 1995). Thirdly, earlier validity theory predominantly focused on the extent to which a test, instrument, or scale measures what it intends to measure, while overlooking

DOI: 10.4324/9781003475729-4

the potential consequences of how scores are interpreted and used (Cureton, 1951; Rulon, 1946).

To address its limitations, Messick (1995) challenged the tripartite perspective on test validity and proposed a redefined concept of validity as a unified construct comprising six distinct dimensions. These dimensions encompass content, substantive, structural, generalizability, external, and consequential aspects. The content dimension pertains to demonstrating the relevance, representativeness, and technical quality of the test, scale, or instrument. It assesses whether a tool effectively captures and reflects the intended construct, as proposed by Lennon (1956) and Messick (1989). The substantive dimension explores the alignment of theoretical underpinnings with observed test responses. It examines whether test takers engage in the expected theoretical processes when responding to assessment tasks, as put forth by Embretson (1983). The structural dimension focuses on the consistency between the scoring structure and the structure of the construct domain under consideration. This aspect, as outlined by Loevinger (1957) and Messick (1989), examines the harmony between how scores are assigned and the underlying structure of the construct. Generalizability, a key facet of construct validity, assesses the extent to which test scores and interpretations can be extrapolated across different sample groups, contexts, and tasks. This dimension, as discussed by Cook and Campbell (1979) and Shulman (1970), evaluates the broader applicability of the assessment. The external dimension concerns the examination of correlations between the test scores and external variables, distinguishing between convergent and discriminant relationships. This aspect, elaborated by Campbell and Fiske (1959), explores a scale's ability to align with related or unrelated external variables. Lastly, the consequential dimension evaluates the potential implications and impact of using test scores for the respondents. It considers the consequences of score utilization (Messick, 1980, 1989).

This chapter's objectives are to assess the psychometric properties of the scale using confirmatory factor analysis (CFA), investigate its associations with theoretically relevant variables via correlation analysis and latent growth curve modelling (LGCM) analysis, and scrutinize the consequences of scale implementation on students' print-based L2 writing. Hence, it concentrates on evaluating the structural, external, and consequential aspects of the construct validity of the scale.

Validating the L2 student DMC competence scale

This section presents the structural, external, and consequential construct validity of the scale.

Structural construct validity

To examine the structural construct validity of the scale, the psychometric properties of the internal structure of the scale were analyzed via CFA based on 263 participants' self-reported scores of L2 student DMC competence. The L2 student DMC competence scale was inserted into a questionnaire, which was posted on the platform *Wenjuanxing*, collecting the students' demographic data like age, gender, and major, and their self-reported DMC competence as measured by the scale. The questionnaire included the Chinese version of the scale to lessen the cognitive load for the participants when providing ratings in relation to the statements for the items of the scale (see Appendix). Regarding the scale items, individuals were asked to rate their level of L2 DMC competence on a 5-point Likert scale (1, 2, 3, 4, or 5 for each item) based on their levels of agreement with the statements. The survey was distributed to students via email and a group on Wechat, a popular messaging and social media platform in mainland China. Students had 20 minutes to finish the survey.

With regard to CFA, prior to conducting the analysis, checks for linearity and normality were completed, and no violation of these assumptions was detected. CFA was then performed by Mplus 8.4. To gauge the model fit, the researcher employed fit indices, as outlined by Kline (2015). These indices included the Chi-Square statistic (χ^2), which assesses the degree of deviation from an ideal or perfect fit. Higher values indicate a less favourable model fit, making it a badness-of-fit statistic. The Comparative Fit Index (CFI) is a goodness-of-fit statistic that compares the degree of deviation in the researcher's model to a null model. It produces values ranging from 0 to 1.0, with the value of 1.0 indicating the most desirable fit. The Tucker–Lewis Index (TLI) operates similarly to CFI by evaluating the relative model fit. Like CFI, values closer to 1.0 are indicative of better fit. The Root-Mean-Square Error of Approximation (RMSEA) is a badness-of-fit statistic measuring the extent of deviation from close or approximate fit. A value of zero represents an ideal fit and is typically reported alongside a 90% confidence interval. The Standardized

60 DMC competence scale validation

Root-Mean-Square Residual (SRMR) is a standardized variant of the root mean square residual (RMR), serving as a measure of the average absolute covariance residual. A perfect model fit is denoted by an RMR of 0, with increasing values indicating a less favourable fit.

The results of the CFA are presented in Figure 4.1.

The inter-factor correlation between *creativity* and *genre awareness* was high, being over 0.95, and item analysis was repeated

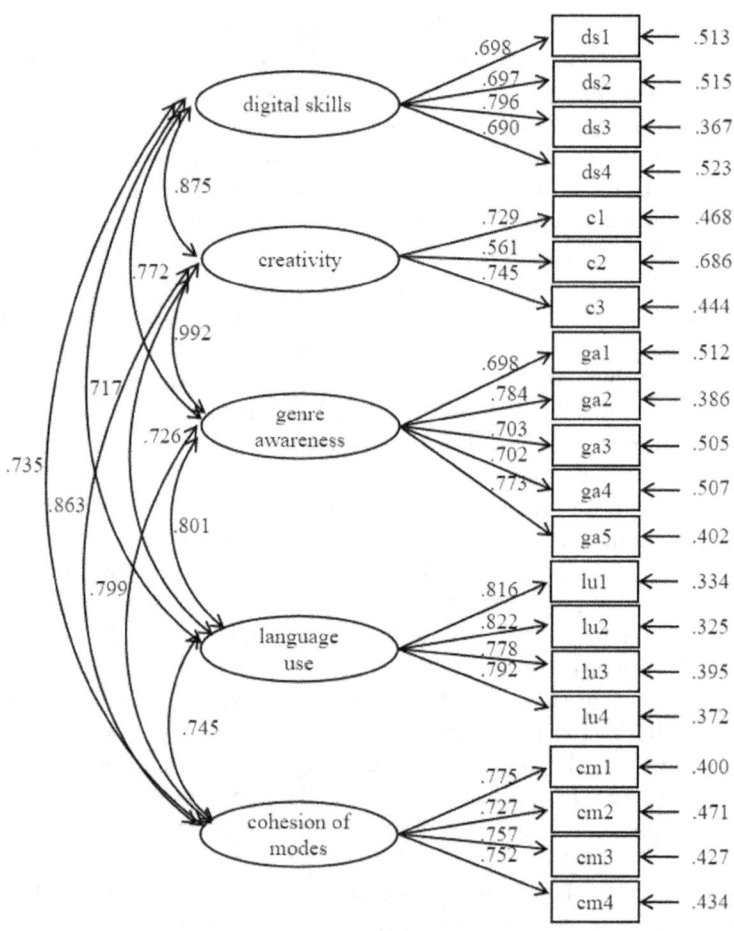

Figure 4.1 The first-order five-factor 20-item model.

to see if there were any problematic items. The model fit indices (i.e., χ^2 = 413.106, df = 160, χ^2/df = 2.582, CFI = 0.916, TLI = 0.900, RMSEA = 0.078, and SMRM = 0.048) showed good model fit. The expert judgment found that *creativity* is too broad to be adequately represented by the three items, and that neither the item *I can assign new meaning to the modes collected from the internet* nor the item *I can give references to the modes* were adequate for this purpose. This left only the item *I can create modes such as drawing, animation, or role-play*, which is insufficient to fully capture this dimension. Therefore, the dimension of *creativity* was eliminated. The item *I can add humour to make my work entertaining to the audience* was also dropped because it was not universally applicable to all genres as humorous writing might not be appropriate for some themes or genres. The item *I can use different organizations according to the genres of my DMC work* and the item *I can use organizations such as introduction-main body-conclusion, cause-effect, compare-contrast, problem-solution, and the like* overlapped, and therefore the item *I can use different organizations according to the genres of my DMC work* was removed due to its lower factor loading compared with the item *I can use organizations such as introduction-main body-conclusion, cause-effect, compare-contrast, problem-solution, and the like*. CFA analysis was conducted to evaluate the resulting four-factor 15-item model, and the model fit indices (χ^2 = 249.142, df = 84, χ^2/df = 2.966, CFI = 0.923, TLI = 0.904, RMSEA = 0.086, and SMRM = 0.050) indicated that the model was suitable. Figure 4.2 shows that the four factors were related but distinct, with inter-factor correlations ranging roughly from 0.7 to 0.8.

The first-order four-factor 15-item model was compared to a second-order model, and the findings revealed that the model fit indices of the second-order model (χ^2 = 249.499, df = 86, χ^2/df = 2.901, CFI = 0.924, TLI = 0.907, RMSEA = 0.085, and SMRM = 0.050) were comparable to those of the first-order four-factor model (see Figure 4.3). The first-order four-factor 15-item model was chosen as the final model, taking into account parsimony, and the final version of the scale is shown in Table 4.1.

A necessary quality for meaningful interpretation and application of test results is reliability (Chung & Baker, 2003). Investigation of the L2 student DMC competence scale's reliability was carried out following the selection of the optimal model. We looked at analyses of the Many-facet Rasch Measurement (MFRM) and Cronbach's alpha.

62 DMC competence scale validation

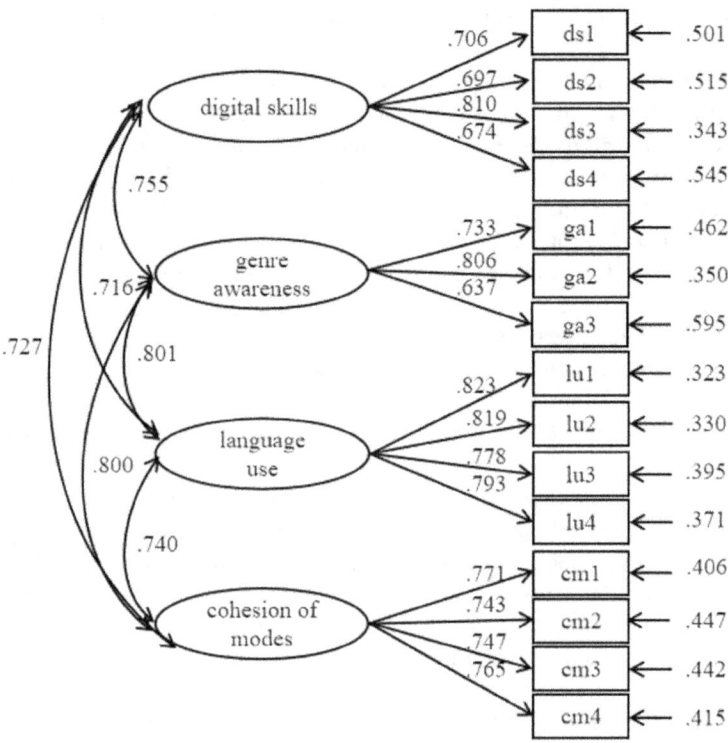

Figure 4.2 The first-order four-factor 15-item model.

A multidimensional Rasch-based model was used on the data set because L2 student DMC competence is a multifaceted construct that encompasses sets of related but different dimensions. The four Rasch models for the L2 student DMC competence scale—*digital skills, genre awareness, language use,* and *cohesion of modes*—explained, respectively, 49.3%, 59.0%, 57.2%, and 57.2% of the total variances, meeting the requirement for unidimensionality of at least 40% of the total variances (Linacre, 2006). This shows that each of the four dimensions measures a single construct.

The mismatch between the observed data and the expected model is indicated by the infit and outfit mean squares values. Linacre (2006) asserts that variation below the cut-off value of 0.5 signifies less

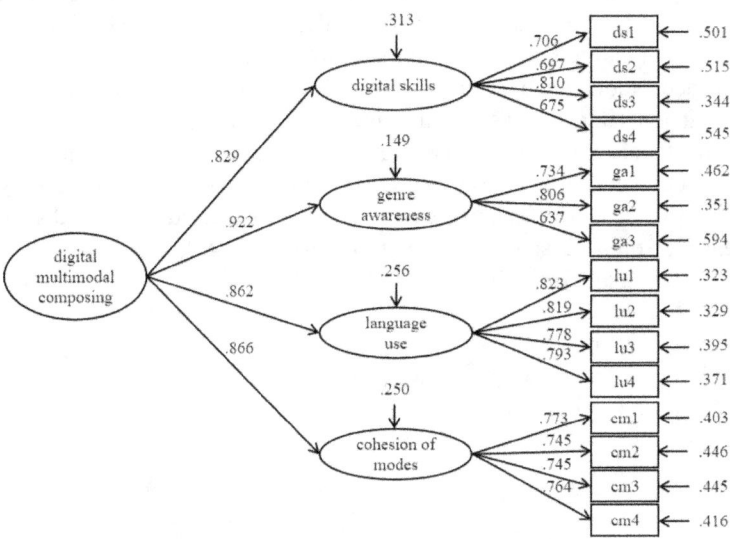

Figure 4.3 The second-order four-factor 15-item model.

Table 4.1 The final version of the L2 student DMC competence scale

---

Digital skills
I know how to edit videos.
I know how to shoot videos.
I know how to do dubbing for the work.
I know how to add special effects to my work.

Genre awareness
I can use organizations such as introduction-main body-conclusion, cause-effect, compare-contrast, problem-solution, and the like.
I can make my work comprehensible to the audience.
I know that works of different genres have different features and styles.

Language use
I can use appropriate tone and intonation in the dubbing of the DMC work.
I can use appropriate stress and pauses in the dubbing of the DMC work.
I can avoid grammatical mistakes in the DMC work.
I can use accurate vocabulary in the DMC work.

Cohesion of modes
I can use modes that relate to the topic of the work.
I can combine modes to achieve cohesion of the meaning.
I can use modes that complement each other to "fill in gaps" in meaning.
I can use modes with similar meanings to reinforce each other.

---

variation than expected, whereas variation around the threshold of 1.5 shows more variation than the model would predict. The findings showed that the infit and outfit mean squares of all items were within the acceptable range (see Figures 4.4, 4.5, 4.6, and 4.7), indicating that the items had a satisfactory fit to the Rasch models.

Category probability curves offer crucial details regarding how the five-point rating scale operates (McNamara, Knoch, & Fan, 2019). The four scale dimensions revealed that there were distinct peaks for each of the five score levels (see Figures 4.8, 4.9, 4.10, and 4.11), suggesting that they all functioned reliably.

ENTRY NUMBER	TOTAL SCORE	TOTAL COUNT	MEASURE	MODEL S.E.	INFIT MNSQ	INFIT ZSTD	OUTFIT MNSQ	OUTFIT ZSTD	PT-MEASURE CORR.	PT-MEASURE EXP.	EXACT MATCH OBS%	EXACT MATCH EXP%	ITEM
4	1037	263	.66	.12	1.15	1.5	1.16	1.6	.78	.82	64.8	61.5	CO3
1	1090	263	-.13	.12	1.10	1.0	1.09	.9	.79	.78	62.4	63.6	CO4
3	1092	263	-.16	.12	.68	-3.6	.68	-3.7	.84	.78	72.9	63.7	CO2
2	1106	263	-.38	.13	1.06	.7	1.04	.5	.76	.77	69.5	64.4	CO1
MEAN	1081.3	263.0	.00	.12	1.00	-.1	.99	-.2			67.4	63.3	
S.D.	26.3	.0	.39	.00	.19	2.0	.19	2.1			4.1	1.1	

Figure 4.4 Infit and outfit statistics of *cohesion of modes*.

ENTRY NUMBER	TOTAL SCORE	TOTAL COUNT	MEASURE	MODEL S.E.	INFIT MNSQ	INFIT ZSTD	OUTFIT MNSQ	OUTFIT ZSTD	PT-MEASURE CORR.	PT-MEASURE EXP.	EXACT MATCH OBS%	EXACT MATCH EXP%	ITEM
3	989	263	.41	.11	1.22	2.2	1.20	2.1	.78	.82	62.9	61.0	GR3
1	1009	263	.14	.12	.92	-.8	.92	-.9	.84	.82	67.2	63.5	GR1
2	1059	263	-.55	.12	.84	-1.7	.83	-1.9	.83	.80	68.6	63.3	GR2
MEAN	1019.0	263.0	.00	.12	.99	-.1	.98	-.2			66.2	62.6	
S.D.	29.4	.0	.41	.00	.16	1.7	.16	1.7			2.4	1.1	

Figure 4.5 Infit and outfit statistics of *genre awareness*.

ENTRY NUMBER	TOTAL SCORE	TOTAL COUNT	MEASURE	MODEL S.E.	INFIT MNSQ	INFIT ZSTD	OUTFIT MNSQ	OUTFIT ZSTD	PT-MEASURE CORR.	PT-MEASURE EXP.	EXACT MATCH OBS%	EXACT MATCH EXP%	ITEM
3	1069	263	.83	.17	1.05	.4	1.02	.2	.86	.87	77.2	76.8	LU3
1	1084	263	.40	.17	1.05	.5	1.00	.0	.85	.86	80.2	77.9	LU1
2	1116	263	-.54	.17	.86	-1.2	.74	-1.9	.85	.85	83.2	78.9	LU2
4	1121	263	-.69	.17	.92	-.7	.85	-1.1	.86	.84	81.2	78.8	LU4
MEAN	1097.5	263.0	.00	.17	.97	-.2	.90	-.7			80.4	78.1	
S.D.	21.7	.0	.63	.00	.08	.7	.11	.9			2.1	.8	

Figure 4.6 Infit and outfit statistics of *language use*.

DMC competence scale validation 65

ENTRY NUMBER	TOTAL SCORE	TOTAL COUNT	MEASURE	MODEL S.E.	INFIT MNSQ	ZSTD	OUTFIT MNSQ	ZSTD	PT-MEASURE CORR.	EXP.	EXACT MATCH OBS%	EXP%	ITEM
3	975	263	.11	.12	1.20	2.1	1.19	2.0	.78	.82	64.8	63.0	DG3
4	979	263	.05	.12	.85	-1.6	.85	-1.7	.83	.82	67.8	62.8	DG4
1	984	263	-.02	.12	.91	-1.0	.91	-1.0	.83	.82	67.4	63.0	DG1
2	992	263	-.13	.12	1.00	.1	.99	-.1	.84	.81	71.2	63.6	DG2
MEAN	982.5	263.0	.00	.12	.99	-.1	.98	-.2			67.8	63.1	
S.D.	6.3	.0	.09	.00	.13	1.4	.13	1.4			2.3	.3	

Figure 4.7 Infit and outfit statistics of *digital skills*.

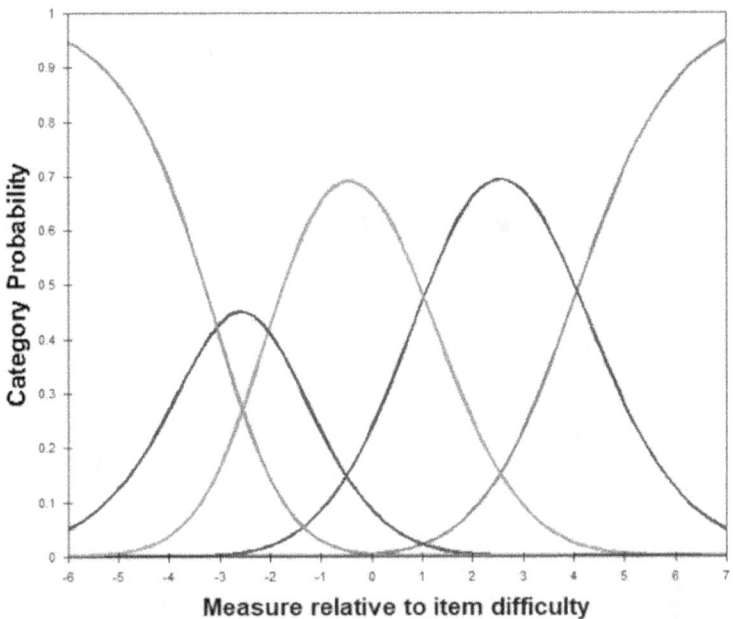

Measure relative to item difficulty

Figure 4.8 Category probability curves for *cohesion of modes*.

Cronbach's alpha values ranged from .758 to .878, exceeding .7, thus demonstrating acceptable reliability (Cortina, 1993; Taber, 2018) (see Table 4.2).

The results showed that the strongest factor was *digital skills*, which was underemphasized in earlier research because most

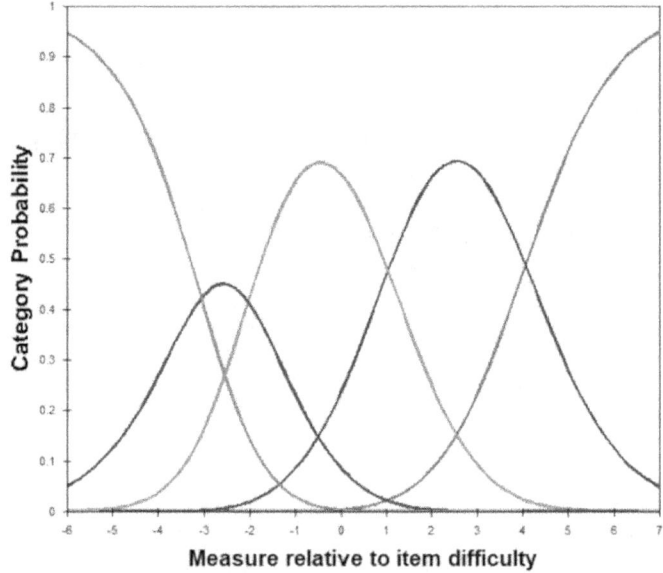

Figure 4.9 Category probability curves for *genre awareness*.

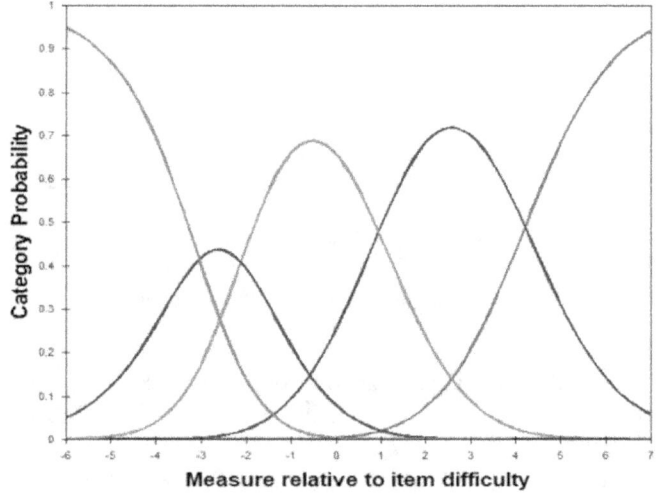

Figure 4.10 Category probability curves for *language use*.

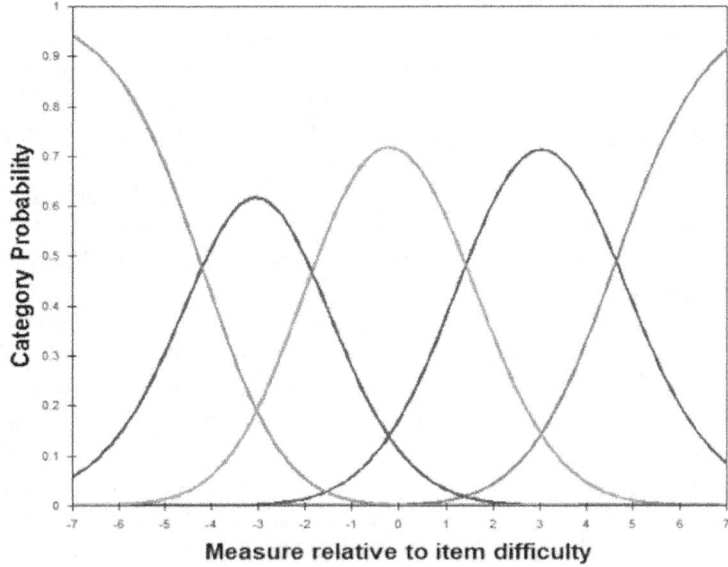

Figure 4.11 Category probability curves for *digital skills*.

Table 4.2 The scale dimensions and reliability indices

Scale Dimensions	α
Digital skills	.841
Genre awareness	.758
Language use	.878
Cohesion of modes	.806

teachers feared that their pupils might become preoccupied with non-linguistic modes rather than the language mode (Jiang & Ren, 2020; Mills & Exley, 2014). *Dubbing* had the highest factor loadings, followed by *editing videos*, *shooting videos*, and *adding special effects to videos*. This suggests that employing *digital skills* to improve L2 learning is possible. For instance, *dubbing* gives L2 students the chance to practise their speaking skills: Before recording their narration, they can practise it in groups or pairs and correct each other's pronunciation.

Genre awareness was the second strongest factor in L2 DMC competence, indicating that constructing specific discourses based on the purpose and audience is a crucial competence in designing DMC works (King, 2021; Smith et al., 2021). Of the sub-dimensions, the item *I can make my work comprehensible to the audience* had the highest factor loading, confirming the earlier findings that engaging the audience is essential for effective DMC works (Bunch & Willett, 2013; Chen & Guan, 2022; Hafner, 2014; Liang, 2019; Liaw & Accurso, 2021; Yeh, 2018).

Language use was the third strongest dimension of L2 student DMC competence, implying that students did not ignore the linguistic mode when designing their DMC works, which may alleviate teachers' concerns about students overemphasizing digital aspects and neglecting the linguistic mode (Jiang & Ren, 2020; Mills & Exley, 2014). This also lent supportive evidence for the potential of DMC in promoting L2 skill development (Hwang et al., 2016; Jiang, 2017; Kim & Belcher, 2020; Tsou et al., 2006; Vandommele et al., 2017; Verdugo & Belmonte, 2007; Yang & Wu, 2012). With regard to the four sub-dimensions of *language use— avoiding grammatical mistakes, using accurate vocabulary, using appropriate tone and intonation in dubbing*, and *using appropriate stress and pause in dubbing*—all exhibited high factor loadings, implying that effective DMC works call for integrated linguistic skills. While DMC is in essence a technology-mediated L2 writing task, speaking plays an indispensable role in enhancing the process of constructing meaning.

Cohesion of modes was the fourth dimension of L2 student DMC competence. The item *Using multiple modes to achieve cohesion of meaning* had the highest factor loadings, implying that combining multiple modes to make cohesive meaning plays a pivotal role in DMC works (Cimasko & Shin, 2017; Hafner, 2014; Park, 2021). *Combining modes in complementary* and *concurrent relationships* also had relatively high factor loadings, dovetailing with earlier findings about the orchestration of modes to achieve cohesion of meaning (Hafner, 2014; Cimasko & Shin, 2017; Park, 2021). *Combining modes in a divergent relationship* is absent from the CFA model, which might be due to its low frequency and difficulty, consistent with Ryu et al. (2022).

External construct validity

The external construct validity of the scale was examined by conducting correlation analysis between students' L2 DMC competence and L2 proficiency, as well as LGCM analysis of the co-development between students' L2 DMC competence and L2 monomodal writing competence.

Correlation analysis

The correlation analysis was performed with SPSS 25.0 software, based on 513 participants' DMC competence scores and L2 proficiency scores, to analyze the relationship between L2 student DMC competence and L2 proficiency. The L2 proficiency of the students was assessed in paper-and-pencil tests in class with two sessions which lasted one and a half hours without reference to dictionaries, textbooks, phones, or any other external sources. The tasks, which were taken from previous final exam papers of the College English I course at the university where the research project was undertaken, included listening (30 marks), reading (30 marks), and writing (30 marks). Multiple-choice questions were used to assess the listening and reading sections. The writing portion required direct writing in response to a prompt. The instructor created a speaking test that required students to read aloud a short passage and respond to two open-ended questions related to the passage, accounting for 30 marks. Hence, the L2 proficiency test had a maximum score of 120 marks. The reading and listening assignments both had an objective score, so the instructor alone rated them. For the writing section, a Ph.D. student in Applied Linguistics from a university on the Chinese mainland who was not the one who coded the data for Research Question 1 evaluated half of the students' scripts for the writing task. In cases where there was a disparity of three marks or more, a discussion was held to resolve the issue. The interrater reliability was 0.798. The remaining writing scripts were subsequently evaluated individually by the instructor. The speaking exam was administered during a single class period, and students were instructed to record themselves reading aloud the passage and their responses to the questions in ten minutes before uploading the audio to the group's Wechat page. The teacher rated the recordings after all had been received. The researcher asked the rater who assisted her in scoring the writing scripts to also evaluate the students' speaking abilities. The interrater reliability was 0.812, and any time there was a three-mark disagreement, a conversation was held to resolve the issue and reach a consensus.

Correlation analysis was performed, with linearity and normality being checked at the beginning. Pearson's correlation coefficient r was calculated to determine whether the scores on the dimensions of L2 student DMC competence after completing all three L2 DMC projects had a significant correlation with the students' overall L2 proficiency assessed by the L2 proficiency test. The results showed that DMC competence measured by the scale closely correlated with the L2 proficiency components, that is, reading, writing, and speaking (see Table 4.3). Three of the DMC competence dimensions were significantly correlated with L2 reading ($r = .119*$ for *genre awareness*, $r = .115*$ for *language use*, $r = .186*$ for *digital skills*) with small effect sizes (Cohen, 1988). All four dimensions were significantly correlated with L2 writing ($r = .194**$ for *cohesion of modes*, $r = .229**$ for *genre awareness*, $r = .246**$ for *language use*, $r = .274**$ for *digital skills*), and the effect sizes were close to medium (Cohen, 1988). All four dimensions were also significantly correlated with L2 speaking ($r = .196**$ for *cohesion of modes*, $r = .147**$ for *genre awareness*, $r = .201**$ for *language use*, $r = .190**$ for *digital skills*), and the effect sizes were small (Cohen, 1988). All four dimensions were also significantly correlated with overall L2 proficiency ($r = .182**$ for *cohesion of modes*, $r = .199**$ for *genre awareness*, $r = .211**$ for

Table 4.3 Correlations between L2 student DMC competence and L2 proficiency

	Listen	Read	Write	Speak	L2	CO	GR	LU	DS
Listen	1	.205**	.219**	.114**	.555**	.003	.031	.001	.018
Read		1	.329**	.313**	.639**	.102	.119*	.115*	.186*
Write			1	.616**	.829**	.194**	.229**	.246**	.274**
Speak				1	.723**	.196**	.147**	.201**	.190**
L2					1	.182**	.199**	.211**	.250**

Note: "Listen" represents "Listening"; "Read" represents "Reading"; "Write" represents "Writing"; "Speak" represents "Speaking"; "L2" represents "L2 proficiency"; "CM" represents "Cohesion of Modes"; "GR" represents "Genre Awareness"; "LU" represents "Language Use"; "DS" represents "Digital Skills".

** p<.01; * p<.0.05

language use, *r* = .250** for *digital skills*), and the effect sizes were small (Cohen, 1988).

As for the correlations among the L2 proficiency components, they were all significantly correlated with each other, and the correlation coefficients ranged from .114** to .829**, suggesting that they were connected but distinguishable.

The correlation analysis revealed a significant correlation between DMC competence as measured by the scale and L2 proficiency in reading, writing, speaking, and overall. This finding supported the scale's external construct validity. The findings were corroborated by prior studies that DMC was associated with overall L2 proficiency (Tsou et al., 2006; Yang & Wu, 2012), L2 reading (Yang & Wu, 2012; Rahimi & Yadollahi, 2017; Yoon, 2013), L2 speaking (Hwang et al., 2016; Jiang, 2017; Somdee & Suppasetseree, 2007), and L2 writing skill development (Kim & Belcher, 2020; Tsou et al., 2006; Vandommele et al., 2017; Yang & Wu, 2012). However, the correlation between L2 DMC competence and L2 listening was insignificant, which might be because collecting modes calls for reading, and recording voiceover and writing scripts are related to L2 speaking and writing, while L2 listening is not a key process in designing DMC works.

LGCM analysis

Based on 513 participants' DMC competence scores and monomodal writing competence scores over three periods of measurement, the relationship between L2 student DMC competence and L2 student monomodal writing competence was analyzed through LGCM using Mplus 8.4 software. After completing each DMC project, the participants were invited to respond to the L2 student DMC competence survey and compose one L2 monomodal essay. They had 30 minutes to produce at least 150 words. The writing assignments' topics were derived from a textbook. The participants' writing abilities were rated on a 5-point holistic scale: 5 excellent, 4 good, 3 average, 2 bad, and 1 very poor. The instructions for the three L2 writing assignments were as follows:

Task 1: Roommates play an important role in your college life. You share your room, your space, and essentially, your life with these people. However, sometimes, you may find it hard to get along well with some roommates. Write at least 150 words within 30 minutes about how to deal with the roommate relationship.

Task 2: With the development of technology, e-commerce is becoming increasingly popular. More and more people prefer to shop online. Write at least 150 words within 30 minutes about the advantages of shopping online.

Task 3: Peer pressure is the type of pressure or influence from your peers that makes you act in a certain way against your will or differently than you usually would. Peer pressure can exert a positive or negative influence on you. Write at least 150 words within 30 minutes about how to deal with peer pressure.

The teacher and the rater who evaluated students' writing and speaking performance in the L2 proficiency test graded the participants' three L2 monomodal writing assignments. The instructor and the Ph.D. student rater each evaluated half of the students' writing samples. In cases where there was a disparity of three marks or more, a discussion was held to settle the difference, and the interrater reliability was 0.801. The remaining writing scripts were subsequently evaluated individually by the instructor.

Before initiating the LGCM analysis, it was imperative to assess both the linearity and normality of the data to ensure its suitability for analysis. LGCM was chosen as the analytical approach due to its capacity to address vital methodological concerns that extend beyond the capabilities of traditional regression methods and mean comparisons. This method acknowledges the dynamic nature of the data, considering repeated measurements as a process that unfolds gradually over time, rather than merely as static points at two distinct time intervals. For each participant in the research project, the researcher used LGCM to track the changes in two time-varying factors—L2 DMC competence and L2 monomodal writing—over time. For L2 DMC competence and L2 monomodal writing, the covariance between intercept factors (i.e., initial level) and slope factors (i.e., the rate of change) was examined to better understand how these two variables developed concurrently over time.

Table 4.4 displays the L2 listening, reading, writing, and speaking scores. The participants' English ability was likely intermediate based on the average of their overall L2 proficiency scores, which was 88.23 (the total score was 120, SD = 9.886). The L2 writing score (M = 21.69, SD = 4.588) and L2 listening score (M = 22.73, SD = 3.493) were the next highest means, respectively. The L2 reading score (M = 24.08, SD = 3.178) was the second lowest. The L2 speaking score (M = 19.73,

Table 4.4 Descriptive statistics of L2 proficiency scores

	Minimum	Maximum	M	SD	Skewness	Kurtosis
Listening	17	30	22.73	3.493	.276	−.591
Reading	10	28	24.08	3.178	−2.411	2.484
Writing	5	30	21.69	4.588	−.783	.541
Speaking	6	25	19.73	2.924	−1.308	2.601
Total	41	107	88.23	9.886	−.974	2.046

Table 4.5 Correlation matrix between DMCs over time

	DMC1	DMC2	DMC3
DMC1		.469**	.424**
DMC2			.531**

Note: "DMC" represents "digital multimodal composing".
** $p<.01$; * $p<.0.05$

Table 4.6 Correlation matrix between MWs over time

	MW1	MW2	MW3
MW1		.233**	.225**
MW2			.259**

Note: "MW" represents "monomodal writing".
** $p<.01$; * $p<.0.05$

SD = 2.924) was the lowest. The findings showed that the participants' receptive abilities were superior to their productive skills. The data appeared to be regularly distributed because the values for skewness and kurtosis were within the range [-2, +2].

As observed in Table 4.5 and Table 4.6, the correlation matrix indicated that correlation coefficients between two adjacent occasions (DMC: .469** and .531**, MW: .233** and .259**) for both DMC competence and monomodal composing competence were higher than those between non-adjacent occasions (DMC: .424**, MW: .225**), providing evidence for the successful estimation of growth curves (Lorenz et al., 2004).

As for the direction and extent of change in DMC competence and monomodal writing competence, all parameter means of the two global factors were statistically significant. The results indicated that DMC competence (MIntercept = 3.982, $p < 0.01$; MSlope = 0.148, $p < 0.01$) and monomodal writing competence (MIntercept = 4.817, $p < 0.01$; MSlope = 1.610, $p < 0.01$) increased over time. The analysis of co-variations in the model showed that the covariance between the intercept factors for DMC and monomodal writing was significant ($r = 0.058$, $p < 0.05$). A similar pattern of significant covariance was observed between the DMC and monomodal writing slope factors ($r = 0.002$, $p < 0.05$) (see Table 4.7), which indicated the existence of a parallel process (co-development) between DMC and monomodal writing at the global factor level.

The LGCM analysis showed that students' DMC competence and monomodal composing competence both showed growth over the course of the semester. Significant covariances were found between both the intercept and slope factors for DMC and monomodal writing, which indicated the existence of a parallel developing process between DMC competence and monomodal writing competence. This result partially agreed with studies (Kim & Belcher, 2020; Rahimi & Yadollahi, 2017; Tsou et al., 2006; Vandommele et al., 2017; Yang & Wu, 2012) that indicated a positive correlation between DMC and monomodal writing. The findings proved that monomodal writing and DMC are two distinct L2 writing tasks, though they do share crucial elements including *organization*, *genre awareness*, and *audience awareness*. Students who are more proficient in monomodal writing are also better at creating meaningful DMC works. In order to help students have a greater knowledge of what writing is and how to learn to write, L2 writing classes can therefore cover both activities.

Consequential construct validity

To inspect the consequential construct validity of the scale, ten participants were randomly chosen for interviews about the impact of the L2 student DMC competence scale on their print-based L2 writing. They were interviewed with the following question: How did the scale affect your traditional English essay writing? The interviews were audio-recorded and transcribed verbatim.

Open and axial coding were employed to analyze the student interview data (Yin, 2016). The researcher was receptive to fresh thoughts

Table 4.7 Results of the parallel process model (PPM)

	Intercept growth factors		Slope growth factors		Correlations among growth factors			
	Mean	Variance	Mean	Variance		I-DMC	I-MW	S-DMC	S-MW
DMC	3.982	0.127**	0.148	0.013**	I-DMC				
MW	4.817	0.454**	1.610	0.111**	I-MW	0.058*			
					S-DMC	0.013*	0.007		
					S-MW	−0.020	−0.167*	0.002*	

Note: "MW" represents "monomodal writing"; "*" represents "$p<0.05$"; "**" represents "$p<0.01$".

and findings that were not covered in the literature and paid attention to everything important to the effect of the L2 student DMC competence scale on students' print-based L2 writing (Mackey & Gass, 2005). Recurrent and prominent themes were identified. Three participants' interviews were coded by a second coder who also assisted with the focus group interviews, and the inter-coder reliability was 0.822. To reach agreement, the differences were discussed one by one. The remaining data were then independently coded by the researchers.

The majority of students revealed that using the scale enabled them to focus on writing elements that are present in both monomodal and multimodal writing. Four of them stated that having a variety of modes allowed them to experiment with different genres in their writing. Christina and Lucy mentioned this:

The scale helps me to think about genres in writing. We usually write argumentations. The scale reminded me to try different genres in future L2 writing practices such as diaries, short novels, speech, and the like to improve my writing competence. (Christina)

We may think of genres while writing English essays. For example, I seldom write narratives in English essays, probably because the genres are usually specified in the test. We often write letters, as you know, letters to Li Hua. We also write some argumentations, but as I can recall, we were not asked to write stories. As a matter of fact, I love stories. I like writing stories in Chinese. The scale reminds me to try different genres in L2 writing. (Lucy)

The students' responses indicated that they were driven to fearlessly communicate their unique and critical opinions through a variety of modes without worrying about receiving poor grades. This was demonstrated by Mia:

When I wrote the roommate relationship essay, I did not write the typical points such as mutual understanding and communication. Instead, I conveyed my idea that if we find it tough to get along with others, we should not make ourselves compromise too much.

Essay writing sample analysis confirmed Mia's point (see Figure 4.12).

DMC competence scale validation 77

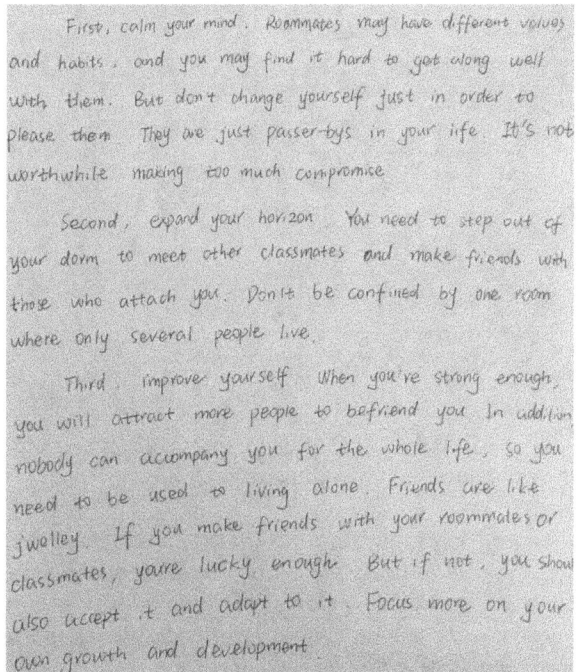

Figure 4.12 Mia's writing sample on the roommate relationship.

Four students stated that they used to be less aware of the audience, and the *audience awareness* scale caused them to recognize the audience's presence and take into account the reactions of their target audience when reading their written texts. They articulated that by using DMC works to target desirable audiences, they might write with greater motivation. Consider Elaine's interview as an example:

> *When I wrote English essays, I seldom thought about the audience. Probably the audience is the rater or teacher who is not close to me and is usually serious. As the scale articulates the existence of an audience in writing, I start to have an awareness of writing for the target audience. For example, I can select my classmates as audiences. In this case, I would feel more relaxed about writing what comes to mind.*

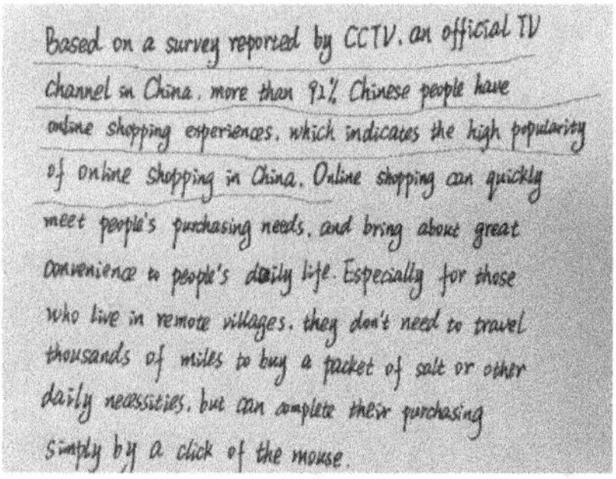

78 *DMC competence scale validation*

> Based on a survey reported by CCTV, an official TV channel in China, more than 92% Chinese people have online shopping experiences, which indicates the high popularity of online shopping in China. Online shopping can quickly meet people's purchasing needs, and bring about great convenience in people's daily life. Especially for those who live in remote villages, they don't need to travel thousands of miles to buy a packet of salt or other daily necessities, but can complete their purchasing simply by a click of the mouse.

Figure 4.13 The use of statistics in Christina's second essay.

Additionally, two students mentioned that *audience awareness* fostered peer evaluation. This was illustrated by Sun:

I used to regard writing as a test task to demonstrate my English proficiency. As my English is poor, I always feel humiliated to let my teachers read my English essays. In designing DMC works, the scale highlights audience awareness. I target my classmates as the audience, so I am more willing to send my essays to peers to ask for their comments and suggestions.

In her essay writing, Christina drew on *cohesion of modes* in the DMC competence scale to bolster her argument. She noted:

The scale tells us to use multiple modes to support our points, which is so enlightening to my essay writing. I need to use textual evidence to support my points.

Writing sample analysis revealed that Christina used statistics to demonstrate the rising popularity of online shopping in China in her second essay (see Figure 4.13).

Two students stated that when writing essays for print-based assignments, they were more mindful of organizations. Eric's illustration of this was as follows:

Previously, when I wrote English essays, I had no awareness of organizing the essay. The only structures I knew were "总-分-总"

DMC competence scale validation 79

and *"总-分" taught by my English teacher. This scale for the DMC project informed me of more structures, that is, cause-effect, compare-contrast, problem-solution, which provides me with more choices.*

Two students stated that when writing essays for print-based assignments, they were more mindful of organizations. Eric mentioned this:

As I am preparing for my IELTS writing, the DMC competence scale drives me to think about the rating scales for the two IELTS writing tasks. Therefore, I downloaded and constantly checked the scales to compare the scale descriptors to my own writing. Knowing the assessment criteria and task expectations reduced my anxiety in preparing for the test, and meanwhile provided me with the right direction to improve my English writing.

In order to support what she revealed in her interviews, Elaine also showed us the rating scale for the International English Language Testing System (IELTS) writing task (see Figure 4.14).

Lucy focused on the self-monitoring and self-revising of the essays, as illustrated by her comments:

Having access to a scale raises my awareness of self-revising the essays. The scale provides goals, and every time I check the scale, I will know where I am, and what I need to do to reach the goals so that I can track my progress of writing development. If I constantly revise the texts based on the requirements, I believe that I will improve my writing abilities from low levels to high levels. Therefore, I really suggest teachers share scales with us when writing English essays.

However, due to difficulty in comprehending and applying the scale criteria as well as rating fatigue, some participants were less positive about the scale's impact on their print-based L2 writing. They expressed a greater preference for examples of writing than the others. This was mentioned by Lydia:

The scale criteria are so abstract, and some of them are hard to understand. Besides, even though I know that those aspects matter,

80 *DMC competence scale validation*

Figure 4.14 The rating scale for the IELTS writing task.

I cannot apply them in my writing because knowing it does not equal being able to do it. I prefer examples to the scale, and we can compare our own writing with example essays, which I believe is more effective in practice writing. I usually just memorize and imitate example essays rather than check the scale to revise my essay.

Anna emphasized the distinction between DMC and print-based L2 writing. She explained:

The scale is tailored to DMC projects rather than English essay writing, so it has minimal effect on my English essay writing.

Rating fatigue was mentioned by Mary and Mina:

There are so many items, and I feel overwhelmed by checking them one by one. (Mary)
It is so tiring to read all items many times. (Mina)

The results of the student interviews suggest that a majority of the participants acknowledged the positive effect of the L2 student DMC competence scale on their monomodal writing, lending support to the consequential construct validity of the scale. They reported that the scale had advantageous effects on their learning of print-based L2 writing. This observation resonated with previous research on the instructional value of scales or rubrics, emphasizing that rubrics have the potential to enhance the quality of students' writing (Andrade, 2001; Andrade & Boulay, 2003; Andrade, Du, & Mycek, 2010; Andrade, Du, & Wang, 2008; Cohen et al., 2002). Furthermore, students displayed a deeper understanding of writing compared to traditional test-oriented writing tasks. They stated that the scale helped them focus on aspects of writing common to both multimodal and monomodal tasks, such as *utilization of multiple modes, organization, genre awareness*, and *audience awareness*. Specific dimensions within the L2 student DMC competence scale, like *cohesion of modes* and *genre awareness*, encouraged students to explore providing evidence within their writing and new genres in print-based L2 writing. This finding supported Timperley and Parr (2009), which suggested that students with access to mastery goals could recognize the deeper features of writing. Additionally, the scale enhanced students' comprehension of the writing process, with students mentioning that it allowed them to practise writing narratives like short novels and diaries. They also suggested that teachers share scales for traditional print-based writing tasks. The scale heightened their metacognitive awareness of self-monitoring and self-revising their print-based L2 writing texts, echoing findings from previous studies (Hawe & Dixon, 2014; Timperley & Parr, 2009). Students expressed increased motivation to write for various purposes, which was consistent with the earlier works of Cumming (2006), Cumming et al. (2002), Lee (2011), and Orsmond et al. (1997), all of which suggest that students become more motivated when learning goals are clear.

While most participants viewed the scale positively, some had a less favourable opinion of its impact on their print-based L2 writing. These students found it challenging to comprehend the scale criteria and preferred having examples. This echoed the important point highlighted by Orsmond et al. (2004) and Wiggins (1998) that students need to understand the scale criteria, and providing examples can facilitate their accurate understanding and interpretation of these criteria. The rating fatigue associated with using the scale resonated with Lee (2017), in which students reported that repeatedly rating interpretations is exhausting. Students' difficulty in applying the scale criteria corroborated Andrade (2001), which concluded that while handing out and explaining rubrics can increase students' knowledge of the writing scale criteria, it is taxing for students to translate the knowledge into actual writing. Furthermore, students pointed out the distinction between DMC and print-based L2 writing, suggesting that they struggled to apply their knowledge across different contexts. This highlights the need to nurture students' competence in transforming knowledge across contexts.

Summary of this chapter

In summary, the L2 student DMC competence scale demonstrated strong construct validity in various aspects. The structural construct validity was supported by the good fit of the four-factor 15-item model in the CFA analyses with good reliability via MFRM analysis and Cronbach's alpha. The external construct validity of the scale was evident through significant correlations between students' L2 DMC competence and L2 proficiency and the co-development between students' L2 DMC competence and L2 monomodal writing competence, as indicated by correlation and LGCM analyses, respectively. Finally, the consequential construct validity of the scale was evidenced by student interviews, which revealed its overall positive impact on students' L2 monomodal writing.

Questions for further discussion

For researchers:

1. What evidence can be collected for the content, substantive, and generalizability construct validity of the L2 student DMC competence scale that has not been investigated in this research project?
2. How can other validity frameworks inform further collection of validity evidence for the L2 student DMC competence scale, such as socio-cognitive validation framework (Weir, 2005; Chalhoub-Deville & O'Sullivan, 2020), assessment use argument (AUA) framework (Bachman & Palmer, 2010), and evidence-centred design (ECD) framework (Mislevy, 2007)?
3. What are other valuable research methods that can be employed to examine the validity of the scale?

For teachers:

1. To what extent does the validity of the L2 student DMC competence scale matter to me when I use it in my implementation of a DMC project?
2. What validity evidence can I possibly obtain from the utilization of the scale in my teaching practice?
3. To what extent do my students' perceptions of using the scale add to the validity evidence for it?

References

Anastasi, A. (1986). Evolving concepts of test validation. *Annual Review of Psychology, 37*, 1–16.
Andrade, H. (2001). The effects of instructional rubrics on learning to write. *Current Issues in Education, 4*(4), 1–21.
Andrade, H., & Boulay, B. (2003). The role of rubric-referenced self-assessment in learning to write. *Journal of Educational Research, 97*(1), 21–34.
Andrade, H., Du, Y., & Mycek, K. (2010). Rubric-referenced self-assessment and middle school students' writing. *Assessment in Education: Principles, Policy & Practice, 17*, 199–214.

Andrade, H., Du, Y., & Wang, X. (2008). Putting rubrics to the test: The effect of a model, criteria generation, and rubric-referenced self-assessment on elementary school students' writing. *Educational Measurement: Issues and Practices*, *27*(2), 3–13.

Angoff, W. H. (1988). Validity: An evolving concept. In: H. Wainer & H. I. Braun (Eds.), *Test validity* (pp. 19–32). Lawrence Erlbaum.

Bachman, L. F. & Palmer, A. S. (2010). *Language assessment in practice*. Oxford University Press.

Bunch, G. C., & Willett, K. (2013). Writing to mean in middle school: Understanding how second language writers negotiate textually-rich content-area instruction. *Journal of Second Language Writing*, *22*, 141–160.

Campbell, D. T., & Fiske, D. W. (1959). Convergent and discriminant validation by the multitrait-multimethod matrix. *Psychological Bulletin*, *56*(2), 81–105.

Chalhoub-Deville, M., & O'Sullivan, B. (2020). *Validity: Theoretical development and integrated arguments*. Equinox Publishing Ltd.

Chen, Y., & Guan, X. Y. (2022). To whom do I write? Chinese EFL test-takers' conceptualization and construction of their audience in the Aptis writing test. In J. Yan. & L. Hamp-Lyons (Eds.), *Assessing the English language writing of Chinese learners of English* (pp. 49–70). Springer.

Chung G. K. W. K., & Baker E. L. (2003). An exploratory study to examine the feasibility of measuring problem-solving processes using a click-through interface. *Journal of Technology, Learning, and Assessment*, *2*(2), 1–29.

Cimasko, T., & Shin, D. (2017). Multimodal resemiotization and authorial agency in an L2 writing classroom. *Written Communication*, *34*(4), 387–413.

Cohen, E., Lotan, R., Scarloss, B., Schultz, S., & Abram, P. (2002). Can groups learn? *Teachers College Record*, *104*(6), 1045–1068.

Cohen, J. (1988). S*tatistical power analysis for the behavioural sciences*. Academic Press.

Cook, T. D., & Campbell, D. T. (1979). *Quasi-experimentation: Design and analysis issues for field settings*. Rand McNally.

Cortina, J. M. (1993). What is coefficient alpha? An examination of theory and applications. *Journal of Applied Psychology*, *78*(1), 98–104.

Cumming, A. (2006). Teaching writing: Orienting activities to students' goals. In E. Uso-Juan & A. Martinez-Flor (Eds.), *Current trends in the development and teaching of the four language skills* (pp. 473–491). Mouton de Gruyter.

Cumming, A., Busch, M., & Zhou, A. (2002). Investigating learners' goals in the context of adult second-language writing. In G. Rijlaarsdam, S. Ransdell, & M. L. Barbier (Eds.), *Studies in writing (Volume 11): New directions for research in L2 writing* (pp. 189–208). Kluwer Academic Publishers.

Cureton, E. E. (1951). Validity. In E. F. Lindquist (Ed.), *Educational measurement* (pp. 621–694). American Council on Education.

Embretson, S. (1983). Construct validity: Construct representation versus nomothetic span. *Psychological Bulletin, 93*, 179–197.

Geisinger, K. F. (1992). The metamorphosis of test validation. *Educational Psychologist, 27*, 197–222.

Hafner, C. A. (2014). Embedding digital literacies in English language teaching: Students' digital video projects as multimodal ensembles. *TESOL Quarterly, 48*, 655–685.

Hawe, E. M., & Dixon, H. R. (2014). Building students' evaluative and productive expertise in the writing classroom. *Assessing Writing, 19*, 66–79.

Hwang, W. Y., Shadiev, R., Hsu, J. L., Huang, Y. M., Hsu, G. L., & Lin, Y. C. (2016). Effects of storytelling to facilitate EFL speaking using Web-based multimedia system. *Computer Assisted Language Learning, 29*(2), 215–241.

Jiang, L. (2017). The affordances of digital multimodal composing for EFL learning. *ELT Journal, 71*(4), 413–422.

Jiang, L. & Ren, W. (2020). Digital multimodal composing in L2 learning: Ideologies and impact. *Journal of Language, Identity & Education, 20*(3), 167–182.

Kim, Y., & Belcher, D. (2020). Multimodal composing and traditional essays: Linguistic performance and learner perceptions. *RELC Journal, 51*(1), 86–100.

King, N. (2021). Designing a better place: Multimodal multilingual composition. In D. Shin, T. Cimasko, & Y. Yi (Eds.), *Multimodal composing in K-16 ESL and EFL education: Multilingual perspectives* (pp. 147–162). Springer.

Kline, R. B. (2015). *Principles and practice of structural equation modeling.* The Guildford Press.

Law, M., & Baum, C. (2005). Measurement in occupational therapy. In M. Law, C. Baum, & W. Dunn (Eds.), *Measuring occupational performance: Supporting best practice in occupational therapy* (pp. 3–20). Slack.

Lee, I. (2011). Bringing innovation to EFL writing through a focus on assessment for learning. *Innovation in Language Learning and Teaching, 5*(1), 19–33.

Lee, I. (2017). *Classroom writing assessment and feedback in L2 school contexts.* Springer.

Lennon, R. T. (1956). Assumptions underlying the use of content validity. *Educational and Psychological Measurement, 16*, 294–304.

Liang, M-Y. (2019). Beyond elocution: Multimodal narrative discourse analysis of L2 storytelling. *ReCALL, 31*(1), 56–74.

Liaw, M. J., & Accurso, K. (2021). Design and opportunity in critical multilingual/multimodal composing pedagogy. In D. Shin, T. Cimasko,

& Y. Yi (Eds.), *Multimodal composing in K-16 ESL and EFL education: Multilingual perspectives* (pp. 89–108). Springer.

Linacre, J. (2006). *A user's guide to Winsteps: Rasch model computer programs*. Winsteps.

Loevinger, J. (1957). Objective tests as instruments of psychological theory. *Psychological Reports, 3*, 635–694.

Lorenz, F. O., Wickrama, K. A. S., & Conger, R. D. (2004). Modeling continuity and change in family relationships with panel data. In R. D. Conger, F. O. Lorenz, & K. A. S. Wickrama (Eds.), *Continuity and change in family relations: Theory, methods, and empirical findings* (pp. 15–62). Lawrence Erlbaum.

Mackey, A., & Gass, S. M. (2005). *Second language research: Methodology and design*. Lawrence Erlbaum.

McNamara, T., Knoch, U., & Fan, J. (2019). *Fairness, justice, and language assessment: The role of measurement*. Oxford University Press.

Messick, S. (1980). Test validity and the ethics of assessment. *American Psychologist, 35*, 1012–1027.

Messick, S. (1989). Validity. In R. L. Linn (Ed.), *Educational measurement* (3rd ed., pp. 13–104). American Council on education and Macmillan.

Messick, S. (1995). Validity of psychological assessment: Validation of inferences from persons' responses and performances as scientific inquiry into score meaning. *American Psychologist, 50*, 741–749.

Mills, K. A., & Exley, B. (2014). Time, space, and text in the elementary school digital writing classroom. *Written Communication, 31*(4), 434–469.

Mislevy, R. J. (2007). Validity by design. *Educational Researcher, 36*, 463–469.

Orsmond, P., Merry, S., & Callaghan, A. (2004). Implementation of a formative assessment model incorporating peer and self-assessment. *Innovations in Education and Teaching International, 41*(3), 273–290.

Orsmond, P., Merry, S., & Reiling, K. (1997). A study in self-assessment: Tutor and students' perceptions of performance criteria. *Assessment & Evaluation in Higher Education, 22*(4), 357–368.

Park, J. H. (2021). "Dear future me": Connecting college L2 writers' literacy paths to an envisioned future self through a multimodal project. In D. Shin, T. Cimasko, & Y. Yi (Eds.), *Multimodal composing in K-16 ESL and EFL education: Multilingual perspectives* (pp. 73–86). Springer.

Rahimi, M., & Yadollahi, S. (2017). Effects of offline vs. online digital storytelling on the development of EFL learners' literacy skills. *Cogent Education, 4*(1), 1285531.

Rulon, P. J. (1946). On the validity of educational tests. *Harvard Educational Review, 16*, 290–296.

Ryu, J., Kim, Y. A., Eum, S., Park, S., Chun, S., & Yang, S. (2022). The assessment of memes as digital multimodal composition in L2 classrooms. *Journal of Second Language Writing, 57*, 100914.

Shulman, L. S. (1970). Reconstruction of educational research. *Review of Educational Research, 40,* 371–396.

Sireci, S. (2009). Packing and unpacking sources of validity evidence: History repeats itself again. In Lissitz, R. W. (Ed.), *The concept of validity: revisions new directions and applications* (pp. 19–38). Information Age Publishing, Inc.

Smith, B. E., Malova, I., & Amgott, N. (2021). Expanding meaning-making possibilities: Bilingual students' perspectives on multimodal composing. In D. Shin, T. Cimasko, & Y. Yi (Eds.), *Multimodal composing in K-16 ESL and EFL education: Multilingual perspectives* (pp. 109–124). Springer.

Somdee, M., & Suppasetseree, S. (2007). Developing English speaking skills of Thai undergraduate students by digital storytelling through websites. *The Foreign Language Learning and Teaching International Conference* (pp. 166–176).

Taber, K. S. (2018). The use of Cronbach's alpha when developing and reporting research instruments in science education. *Research in Science Education, 48*(6), 1273–1296.

Timperley, H. S., & Parr, J. M. (2009). What is this lesson about? Instructional processes and student understandings in writing classrooms. *The Curriculum Journal, 20*(1), 43–60.

Tsou, W., Wang, W., & Tzeng, Y. (2006). Applying computer multimedia storytelling Website in foreign language learning. In *Proceedings 3rd IEEE International Conference on Advanced Technologies* (pp. 262–263).

Vandommele, G., Van den Branden, K., Van Gorp, K., & De Maeyer, S. (2017). In-school and out-of-school multimodal writing as an L2 writing resource for beginner learners of Dutch. *Journal of Second Language Writing, 36,* 23–36.

Verdugo, D. R., & Belmonte, I. A. (2007). Using digital stories to improve listening comprehension with Spanish young learners of English. *Language Learning & Technology, 11*(1), 87–101.

Weir, C. J. (2005). *Language testing and validation: An evidence-based approach.* Macmillan.

Wiggins, G. (1998). *Educative assessment: Designing assessments to inform and improve student performance.* Jossey-Bass.

Yang, Y. F., & Wu, W. I. (2012). Digital storytelling for enhancing student academic achievement, critical thinking, and learning motivation: A year-long experimental study. *Computers & Education, 59*(2), 339–352.

Yeh, H-C. (2018). Exploring the perceived benefits of the process of multimodal video making in developing multiliteracies. *Language Learning & Technology, 22*(2), 28–37.

Yin, R. K. (2016). *Qualitative research from start to finish* (2nd ed.). The Guilford Press.

Yoon, T. (2013). Are you digitized? Ways to provide motivation for ELLs using digital storytelling. *International Journal of Research Studies in Educational Technology, 2*(1), 25–34.

Yun, J., & Ulrich, D. A. (2002). Estimating measurement validity: A tutorial. *Adapted Physical Activity Quarterly, 19*, 32–47.

英语多模态写作能力调查

本研究旨在了解中国大学生的英语多模态写作能力。选项答案没有正确错误之分。

该问卷通常完成时间为10分钟。问卷结果仅用作学术研究，所有数据会保密化处理，不会泄露个人信息。如果对本研究有任何疑问或有兴趣进一步了解，请联系yb97712@um.edu.mo。

姓名：
学号：
年龄：
性别：
专业：

请对以下表述进行评分：5非常同意，4同意，3一般，2不同意，1非常不同意

1. 我会在配音中使用恰当的语音和语调。
2. 我知道如何剪辑视频。
3. 我可以使用跟主题相关的模态。
4. 我可以使用多种结构，比如引入-主体-结论、因-果、比较-对比、问题-方案等。
5. 我知道如何拍摄视频。
6. 我可以使用多种具有相似意义的模态，使其互相加强。
7. 我知道如何在作品中加入特效。
8. 我可以通过绘画、动画或者表演等创造模态。
9. 我可以为模态提供出处。
10. 我知道不同体裁的英语多模态写作有不同的特点和风格。
11. 我可以在多模态作品中避免语法错误。
12. 我知道如何为我的作品配音。
13. 我可以使我的多模态作品被观众理解。
14. 我可以在我的多模态作品中加入幽默的元素来使观众觉得有趣。
15. 我可以把所搜集的模态整合起来以使意义连贯。
16. 我可以在配音中使用恰当的重音和停顿。
17. 我可以使用多种不同意义的模态，使其互相补充。
18. 我会在多模态写作中尽量保证单词拼写正确。
19. 我会根据多模态作品的体裁来使用不用的结构。
20. 我可以赋予从网上搜到的模态新的意义。

5 Scale utilization for assessing L2 student digital multimodal composing competence

Introduction

Assessment as learning (AaL) refers to "a process through which pupil involvement in assessment can feature as part of learning" (Dann, 2002, p.153), which accentuates the central role of students in assessment, such as self- and peer assessment (Gardner, 2006), and regards assessment as a process of fostering student metacognition (Earl, 2013) and students as the connector between assessment and learning (Earl & Katz, 2006). While Lee (2017) called on teachers to implement AaL in technology-enhanced L2 writing tasks, few studies have heeded the call and realized the AaL practices in such tasks as DMC. Following the development and validation of the L2 student DMC competence scale in Chapter 3 and Chapter 4, respectively, this chapter covers the scale being put into use in the L2 classroom as an AaL tool to guide students' self- and peer-assessment practices in a DMC project.

From the 313 participants involved in this research project who designed three DMC artifacts over the semester in the College English I course, five participants were interviewed and observed for their self- and peer-assessment processes. The rationale for selecting them was that they had relatively high L2 proficiency (M = 83.8, SD = 2.4) for the cohort, based on the assessment test at the beginning of the semester, and they showed high motivation in the DMC project and produced high-quality DMC works. To ensure a diverse participant pool, the students were chosen from various groups and majors. To ensure confidentiality and anonymity, all participants were assigned pseudonyms.

DOI: 10.4324/9781003475729-5

Teachers' use of the L2 student DMC competence scale

The instructor utilized the scale in the College English I course, and she first provided self- and peer-assessment training to students and asked them to conduct self- and peer assessment.

Self- and peer-assessment training

Both a printed version and an electronic version of the L2 student DMC competence scale were distributed to the participants to guide their self-assessment activities (see Table 5.1). To prepare participants

Table 5.1 The DMC self-assessment sheet

I can	5	4	3	2	1
Digital skills					
1. I know how to edit videos.					
2. I know how to shoot videos.					
3. I know how to do dubbing for the work.					
4. I know how to add special effects to my work.					
Genre awareness					
5. I can use organizations such as introduction-main body-conclusion, cause-effect, compare-contrast, problem-solution, and the like.					
6. I can make my work comprehensible to the audience.					
7. I know that works of different genres have different features and styles.					
Language use					
8. I can use appropriate tone and intonation in the dubbing of the DMC work.					
9. I can use appropriate stress and pauses in the dubbing of the DMC work.					
10. I can avoid grammatical mistakes in the DMC work.					
11. I can use accurate vocabulary in the DMC work.					
Cohesion of modes					
12. I can use modes that relate to the topic of the work.					
13. I can combine modes to achieve cohesion of the meaning.					
14. I can use modes that complement each other to "fill in gaps" in meaning.					
15. I can use modes with similar meanings to reinforce each other.					

for self-assessment, the instructor conducted one session of training. During this session, the instructor explained the concept of self-assessment, clarified the distinction between self-assessment and self-rating, and elucidated the advantages of and steps involved in the self-assessment process. Drawing on the work of Lee (2017) and Xiang et al. (2021), the training covered all the criteria and descriptors included in the DMC competence scale. The instructor explained the assessment criteria covering *digital skills*, *genre awareness*, *language use*, and *cohesion of modes,* and provided explicit instruction on how to meet the criteria by exhibiting and analyzing representative DMC samples, which had been created by the instructor's and her colleagues' previous students. For example, for *cohesion of modes*, students were instructed to either make texts, images, and sounds complement each other by expressing differing information or make texts, images, and sounds reinforce each other by conveying similar information. Following the training, participants were encouraged to utilize the scale at various stages—before, during, and after designing their DMC artifacts. They were instructed to employ the scale to gather information about their DMC performance, evaluate and reflect on the quality of their DMC artifacts, identify their strengths and weaknesses, and make revisions to enhance their work.

For the peer feedback training, informed by Min (2005), the instructor provided one session of training on a four-step procedure, namely: "Clarifying writers' intentions, identifying the source of problems, explaining the nature of problems, and making specific suggestions" (p. 123). Through a sample of peer feedback, the instructor modelled 1) how to clarify the writers' intention by asking "Do you mean..." or "Are you saying...", 2) how to identify and explain a problem by logically providing reasons for why the area was problematic, and 3) how to provide specific suggestions by providing corrections or solutions to address the problem. The participants were encouraged to utilize the scale for peer assessment at various stages—before, during, and after designing their DMC artifacts. The instructor then gave the DMC peer-assessment sheet to the students (see Table 5.2).

Scale-referenced self-assessment

The students were engaged in a cyclical process of self-assessment with a variety of micro-processes in the DMC project, i.e., *determining*

Table 5.2 The DMC peer-assessment sheet

My classmate can:	5	4	3	2	1

Digital skills
1. edit videos.
2. shoot videos.
3. do dubbing for the work.
4. add special effects to the work.

Genre awareness
5. use organizations such as introduction-main body-conclusion, cause-effect, compare-contrast, problem-solution, and the like.
6. make his/her work comprehensible to the audience.
7. show different features and styles for works of different genres.

Language use
8. use appropriate tone and intonation in the dubbing of the DMC work.
9. use appropriate stress and pauses in the dubbing of the DMC work.
10. avoid grammatical mistakes in the DMC work.
11. use accurate vocabulary in the DMC work.

Cohesion of modes
12. use modes that relate to the topic of the work.
13. combine modes to achieve cohesion of the meaning.
14. use modes that complement each other to "fill in gaps" in meaning.
15. use modes with similar meanings to reinforce each other.

performance criteria, self-directed feedback seeking, self-reflection, and *taking action.*

Determining performance criteria

Three of the five students admitted that they referred to the criteria in the scale, such as *digital skills*, but did not pay close attention to the descriptors because they had their own conceptions of DMC competence based on prior or current learning experiences. Peter, for instance, stated:

The scale is just a reference. I have more ideas about what good DMC work looks like based on my previous experience of making videos. I am a big fan of making and sharing vlogs in Douyin (the Chinese version of TikTok). *To make sure my videos receive more "likes" from my fans, I have made great efforts by taking online courses and consulting with Little Red Book to learn video editing skills.*

Allen demonstrated how his knowledge from other pertinent courses enhanced his comprehension of DMC competence. He stated:

I am enrolled in another course named Multimedia Technology in which I am also studying how to make and edit videos. My understanding of the criteria to judge DMC works is also based on what I learned in that course. This project offers a golden opportunity for me to apply what I have learned.

Classroom observations of the peer and self-feedback confirmed that, in addition to the five criteria from the scale, Peter and Allen also focused on other criteria such as the delivery of the videos. This is illustrated by the following quote:

The flow of some scenes is not fluid enough, and one transition lasts for nearly five seconds. (Allen)

Allen's representation mirrored the DMC sample analysis, which showed a four-second pause (see Figure 5.1).

However, Rachel and Olivia showed a different pattern from the other three. They revealed that the scale helped them to observe and understand what was required of them by breaking down the DMC performance requirements into particular descriptors. They noted the following:

We paid close attention to all the requirements in the scale and tried our best to meet them. (Rachel)

The descriptors are detailed explanations of the scale criteria, which are useful for us to understand and internalize the task expectations. (Olivia)

The majority of the interviewees stated that their performance criteria were not fixed but were calibrated by peer samples, comments,

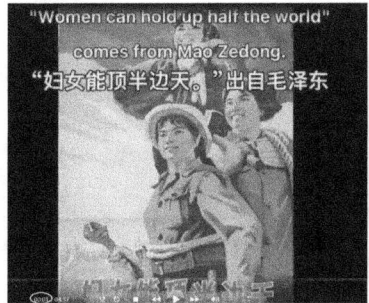 

Figure 5.1 The four-second pause in the DMC work.

and their own analysis of the DMC samples following each DMC project. For instance, Allen pointed out:

We did not adopt the same criteria for the three DMC projects. In the first project, we had no access to the scale, so we just relied on our own understanding of what good DMC works look like. In the second project, we not only referred to the scale, but also added our own understanding of DMC works. In the third project, we enriched the criteria by incorporating some features from other group samples and our classmates' suggestions for us, such as the perspectives of shooting videos, the clarity, and the amusement of the videos.

Self-directed feedback seeking

The five students all stated that they looked for both internal and external feedback. They sought out external feedback from group members after drawing on internal feedback to make modifications, as demonstrated by Rachel:

In the second project, my job was dubbing. I recorded my narration and listened to it by myself first. I felt it was not good enough, so I redid it. After several times, when I was satisfied with my work, I read it aloud to all the other four members to ask for their feedback about my pronunciation, emotion, pace, and the like.

96 DMC competence scale utilization

Figure 5.2 The feedback report generated by *Pigai* for Emma's group's script.

They also consulted with the automatic essay scoring system *Pigai* to check their vocabulary and grammar, which is also inquiry external feedback. Emma stated:

After we peer-reviewed the scripts, we usually input them into Pigai to check if there were lexical or grammatical mistakes that we failed to locate.

Emma's observation matched the feedback report *Pigai* produced (see Figure 5.2).

All five of the students obtained external feedback through monitoring, such as comparing their DMC works with earlier ones. Olivia stated:

DMC competence scale utilization 97

After each DMC work was displayed in class, I would reflect on the drawbacks of the work, and set goals to overcome them in the next project. I wish to make breakthroughs in the next work.

Most of them revealed that the L2 student DMC competence scale was a reference against which they obtained external monitoring feedback to evaluate the quality of the DMC works. As noted by Emma and Peter, they focused on the criteria of the scale to evaluate the quality of the DMC works.

Self-reflection

Most of the students confirmed that they would evaluate the merits and shortcomings of their works against the L2 student DMC competence scale. Emma stated:

We would reflect on the strengths and weaknesses in each DMC work against the criteria of the DMC self-assessment scale. We then focused more on the weaknesses and attempted to break through in the next work.

Four of them articulated that they would carefully consider the feedback from the group members or *Pigai*. If the feedback was reasonable, they would incorporate and act on it. However, if they disagreed with the feedback, they would discuss it with each other until they reached a consensus. Olivia's remark serves as an example:

If I was sceptical about some comments, I would discuss them with my peers, and consult dictionaries or the internet to determine whether the feedback was accurate or not. The same is true for the feedback from Pigai.

Taking action

The students reported that the self-assessment data helped them go beyond the DMC competence scale and define new learning objectives and assist them in revising and improving their DMC works, as well as updating their knowledge of DMC competence and improving their performance standards. Rachel pointed out:

> *The self-assessment information was the feedback for our work. We followed those suggestions to revise and improve our work. Meanwhile, it also enriched our understanding of DMC beyond the scale. For example, at first, we paid less attention to the audience engagement (there is only one descriptor addressing audience comprehension). After incorporating feedback from peers' samples, we realized that making the work entertaining to the audience was so important. Therefore, we aimed to add humorous elements to our work the next time.*

The amusing elements in their DMC work mentioned by Rachel were corroborated by their DMC sample analysis in which a "小瘪三" (which means "rascal" in English) violated the quarantine policy by attempting to get out of the house through windows during COVID-19, but was caught and immediately censured by others. His movements were so timid that they aroused laughter from the whole class (see Figure 5.3).

Allen also said that after viewing his peers' works, he had a greater grasp of other genres:

> *Watching my classmates' works made me realize that genres matter in DMC projects. Some groups made TV programmes, and some made mini-films, and I found that this was so inspiring, which drove me to consider trying debating or speech in the next project and trying new genres in future works in Douyin.*

Allen's comment about experimenting with different genres was in line with the DMC sample analysis, which highlighted the speech genre (see Figure 5.4).

The students' self-assessment practices resembled the cyclical model described in Yan and Brown (2017). The scale helped them *determine performance criteria*, but they tended to derive criteria from both the DMC competence scale and their personal understanding of DMC competence. They also drew on the scale descriptors as monitoring feedback, with peer samples and comments in tandem with *Pigai* comments complementing them to maximize the learning potential of feedback. The scale also caused students to *reflect on* the strengths and weaknesses of their DMC works, and all self-assessment information would contribute to their DMC competence understanding, which usually extended beyond the scale descriptors.

DMC competence scale utilization 99

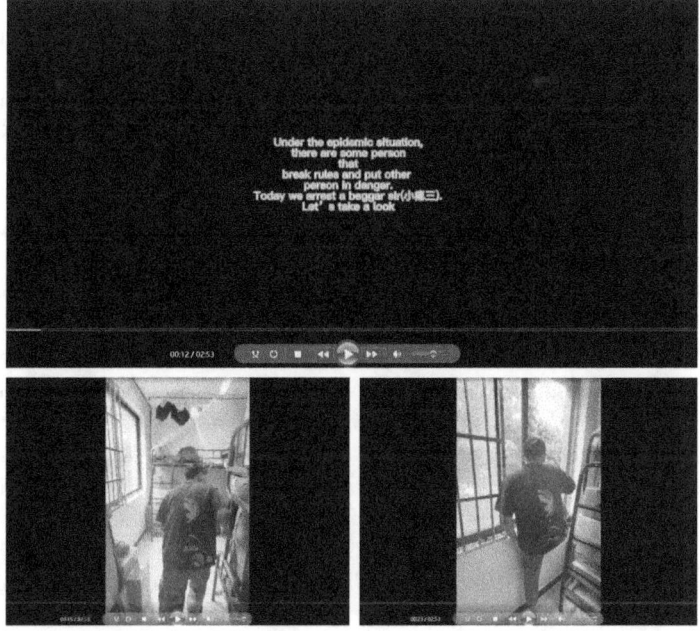

Figure 5.3 Humorous elements in Rachel's DMC group work.

Figure 5.4 The genre of speech in Allen's DMC group work.

100 DMC competence scale utilization

Scale-referenced peer assessment

Some students noted that after finishing their part of the work, they would draw on the scale to conduct peer assessment within their groups to provide comments on each other's work. Afterwards, they sought peer feedback from other groups to refine their works. This was exemplified by Emma:

> As we divided the labour in the DMC project, we would first draw on the scale to provide feedback on each other's work. For instance, in one DMC project, my job was to write the script. After we combined our parts to form one whole, we arranged a meeting to provide comments on each other's work. The group members reviewed my writing and pointed out the grammatical, lexical, and organizational mistakes. They also provided me with suggestions on the interaction with the audience, and to use language that is interesting to the audience. For example, one peer advised me to use "you", the second-person singular pronoun, more to engage the audience. After we conducted within-group peer assessment, we revised our parts and then combined them together. We would then ask peers in other groups to have a look and identify any problems that we had failed to find. For instance, after our second DMC project, we sent the work to John. He detected one typo that we did not notice, and he also noted that on some scenes, the narration was overwhelmed by the soundtrack.

Olivia noted that the peer feedback together with example demonstrations aided her revision of the DMC works. She commented:

> I was once responsible for dubbing. I recorded my narration and then listened to it multiple times based on the scale criteria, i.e., pace, intonation, stress, and pauses. I realized that there were few pauses and stresses, sounding sort of tedious. Therefore, I turned to my classmate whose spoken English is excellent to solicit her comments. She gave me suggestions, such as marking key words or phrases, slowing the pace, and modulating volume. She also read the script for demonstration. I recorded and listened to her narration over and over again. I feel that her suggestions combined with her demonstration helped me a lot. The final result was not bad.

DMC competence scale utilization 101

This combination of the scale and examples was echoed by Peter:

The scale was undoubtedly helpful in providing peer feedback. However, sometimes, the descriptors could only guide us to find problems, but for solutions, examples might be more useful. As you shared with us all the DMC samples from the classes you taught, I watched them often and also associated the scale descriptors with the DMC samples. If works were good illustrations of the descriptors, I would send them to my group members or classmates to demonstrate my suggestions.

Peter also reported that the scale descriptors helped him to formulate checklist questions to evaluate his peers' works, such as "Is the work comprehensible to the audience?", and "Is the language accurate in its vocabulary and grammar?"

Rachel articulated that they would focus on the criteria that are product-oriented, such as *language use*, *cohesion of modes*, and *genre awareness*. *Digital skills* was used more for process-oriented self-assessment. This was illustrated by Rachel:

The scale made our peer assessment more intentional and purposeful. When I provided peer feedback, I tended to check the scale descriptors one by one. But not all descriptors were relevant: For example, in digital skills, "I know how to edit videos", "I know how to shoot videos", and "I know how to do dubbing for the work", they were more suitable for self-assessment. I usually omitted them from peer assessment. Other descriptors were relevant and guided my peer assessment.

Allen mentioned that in addition to the DMC competence scale, he would also pay attention to minor aspects, such as layout, font, transitions, clarity of the images, and references. He commented:

In providing peer feedback, I tended to focus on more than the aspects mentioned in the scale. I emphasized the quality of the product more, and would provide suggestions on layout, the size and colour of fonts, transitions, and clarity of the images.

Classroom observation of peer assessment resonated with his interviews. He put more emphasis on the delivery of the DMC work, and suggested avoiding using a white colour font when the background was also white and trying to use higher-definition images.

The student interviews and the observations of peer assessment in class showed that most students drew on the scale to provide feedback. They would evaluate their peers' group works against the scale descriptors and formulate checklist questions based on the scale. They revealed that the combination of the scale and examples facilitated effective DMC peer assessment. However, some students tended to go beyond the scale and provide feedback based on their own understanding of DMC competence, while others focused only on the scale criteria that they felt were relevant to provide peer feedback.

Teacher reflection on use of the scale in the DMC project

Before the concept of L2 student DMC competence was introduced to students (in the first DMC project), while the instructor emphasized that DMC was a technology-enhanced L2 writing task, many students viewed it as a video assignment and tried to make their videos fancy and perfect rather than focusing on their writing. Some even turned to automated systems to translate Chinese scripts into English. Being aware of the students' misinterpretation of the DMC project, possibly due to their unfamiliarity with the task, the instructor realized that the learning goals and success criteria of the DMC project needed to be made more transparent to them, and their DMC design process also needed to be assessed. She wrote in her journal on October 25, 2021: "Most students are still unclear about the requirements of the DMC project. I need to tell them how their works are graded. They care about scores." After providing them with the scale, the situation improved in the next DMC project. Several groups sent the instructor the scripts for review, and she noticed that the scripts were written by the students themselves rather than being translated by automated translation programs. An inspection of their DMC works revealed that the number of inaccurate expressions had decreased, and irrelevant modes were used less, which had been common problems in the first DMC project. After each DMC project, the instructor displayed the students' works in class and invited them to provide self- and peer feedback. She noticed that after being provided with the scale, the students' feedback became more focused on the scale descriptors. She was heartened by students' attempts to utilize the scale to assist them in developing a better understanding of the DMC task expectations and requirements.

The scale-referenced self-assessment and peer assessment are interwoven with each other, as the sub-process "self-directed feedback seeking" involves peer feedback (Yan & Brown, 2017). By using the scale as a self- and peer-assessment tool, students became more metacognitively aware of the DMC competence they needed to develop, so they could set their own goals based on the scale, monitor progress toward these goals, and determine how to bridge any gaps (Andrade et al. 2012; Deng et al., 2023; Lam, 2010; Lee et al., 2019). Some students viewed the scale as a reference for their own understanding of DMC competence and their prioritized criteria, indicating that they personalized the learning goals according to their own situations (Lee, 2017). Identifying their needs and seeking feedback from peers purposefully and proactively on areas where they needed help indicated that students' learner autonomy improved through scale-referenced self- and peer assessment (Earl, 2013; James, 2006; Klenowski, 2009; Marshall & Drummond, 2006). Students also found the scale useful in forming metacognitive questions to evaluate their peers' works and provide comments, suggesting that their metacognition was enhanced by the scale-referenced peer assessment (Lee et al., 2019). By combing the DMC scale and DMC samples to facilitate peer assessment, students could have a more precise understanding of DMC assessment (Orsmond et al., 1997; Wiggins, 1998) and serve as learning resources for each other (Lee, 2017; Lee et al., 2019).

Summary and implications of this chapter

This chapter has investigated the utilization of the L2 student DMC competence scale in the L2 classroom and found that the scale can effectively guide students' self- and peer-assessment practices. It has identified that students drew on the scale to *determine performance criteria* and guide their *self-directed feedback seeking* and *self-reflection* (Yan & Brown, 2017). They also referred to the scale descriptors to provide and seek peer feedback. This research marks a departure from the traditional approach of assessing DMC projects solely from an assessment of learning (AoL) perspective, and examines the self- and peer-assessment practices of L2 student writers in DMC projects. Further studies are needed to explore the impact of self- and peer assessment on students' L2 writing practices in more depth. Additionally, while this chapter has reported scale-referenced self- and peer-assessment practices in DMC, the focus of the research project was self-assessment. Therefore, future studies could further study scale-referenced peer assessment in DMC. Furthermore, other factors that affect students' self- and peer-assessment practices in DMC projects, such as language proficiency, motivation, learner agency, and self-regulation, are not examined in this book and warrant future study.

From a pedagogical perspective, the implementation of AaL in technology-enhanced L2 writing tasks serves as a valuable example for educators in similar contexts. It encourages teachers to consider integrating student assessment practices into their own classrooms. As the utilization of the DMC scale plays an important role in student self- and peer assessment, it might heighten teachers' awareness of the instructional values of scales and motivate them to use scales in their formative assessment practices to make transparent the learning goals and task expectations to students and guide their self-assessment practices.

Questions for further discussion

For teachers:

1. How can the L2 student DMC competence scale facilitate my AaL practice in class?
2. Apart from self- and peer assessment, what role(s) can the scale play in my AaL-focused classroom?
3. What interventions can be implemented to improve the learning potential of the scale?
4. To what extent does using the scale heighten my students' metacognition and learning autonomy?
5. What are the difficulties and challenges of implementing AaL in the L2 classroom?
6. What are the difficulties and challenges for students using the scale in DMC self- and peer assessment?

For researchers:

1. What is the effect of using the scale on students' DMC performance?
2. What is the effect of using the scale on students' monomodal writing performance?

3. How can I quantitatively analyze the impact of L2 proficiency on students' self- and peer assessment with the L2 student DMC competence scale?
4. To what extent does feedback literacy affect students' DMC self- and peer-assessment practices?
5. Can the scale be used for diagnostic writing assessment? If so, how?

References

Andrade, H., Huff, K., & Brooke, G. (2012). *Assessing learning: The students at the center series*. The Nellie Mae Education Foundation.

Dann, R. (2002). *Promoting assessment as learning: Improving the learning process*. Routledge.

Deng, Y., Liu, D., & Feng, D. (2023). Students' perceptions of peer review for assessing digital multimodal composing: The case of a discipline-specific English course. *Assessment & Evaluation in Higher Education*. Advanced online publication.

Earl, L. M. (2013). Assessment for learning; Assessment as learning: Changing practices means changing beliefs. In Hong Kong Education Bureau (Ed.). *Assessment and Learning* (issue 2) (pp. 1–5). The Hong Kong Government Printer.

Earl, L. M., & Katz, S. (2006). R*ethinking classroom assessment with purpose in mind*. Government of Alberta, British Columbia, Manitoba, Northwest Territories, Nunavut, Saskatchewan, and Yukon Territory: Western and Northern Canadian Protocol for Collaboration in Education.

Gardner, J. (2006). *Assessment and learning*. Sage.

James, M. (2006). Assessment, teaching and theories of learning. In J. Gardner (Ed.), *Assessment and Learning* (pp. 47–60). Sage.

Klenowski, V. (2009). Assessment for learning revisited: An Asia-Pacific perspective. *Assessment in Education: Principles, Policy and Practice*, *16*(3), 263–268.

Lam, R. (2010). A peer review training workshop: Coaching students to give and evaluate peer feedback. *TESL Canada Journal*, *27*(2), 114–127.

Lee, I. (2017). *Classroom assessment and feedback in L2 school contexts*. Springer.

Lee, I., Mak, P., & Yuan, R. E. (2019). Assessment as learning in primary writing classrooms: An exploratory study. *Studies in Educational Evaluation*, *62*, 72–81.

Marshall, B., & Drummond, M. J. (2006). How teachers engage with assessment for learning: Lessons from the classroom. *Research Papers in Education*, *21*(2), 133–149.

Min, H. T. (2005). Training students to become successful peer reviewers. *System*, *33*(2), 293–308.

Orsmond, P., Merry, S., & Reiling, K. (1997). A study in self-assessment: Tutor and students' perceptions of performance criteria. *Assessment & Evaluation in Higher Education, 22*(4), 357–368.

Wiggins, G. (1998). *Educative assessment: Designing assessments to inform and improve student performance.* Jossey-Bass.

Xiang, X., Yuan, R., & Yu, B. (2021). Implementing assessment as learning in the L2 writing classroom: A Chinese case. *Assessment & Evaluation in Higher Education, 47*(5), 727–741.

Yan, Z., & Brown, G. T. L. (2017). A cyclical self-assessment process: Towards a model of how students engage in self-assessment. *Assessment & Evaluation in Higher Education, 42*(8), 1247–1262.

6 Conclusion

What knowledge and insights are provided in this book?

Drawing on the related literature and the empirical data from student focus group interviews, classroom observations, and DMC sample analysis, L2 student DMC competence was found to be a multidimensional concept that encompasses *utilization of multiple modes*, *genre awareness* (with the subcategory of *audience awareness*), *digital skills*, *creativity*, *delivery*, *cohesion*, *identity expression*, *language use* (with the subcategory of *linguistic choices*), and *organization*.

Based on the L2 student DMC competence model, a nine-factor 45-item L2 student DMC competence scale was developed. To ensure the validity of the scale, evidence was collected in the three key areas of structural, external, and consequential construct validity. The structural construct validity of the scale was assessed, and it was determined that the best-fit model consisted of a first-order structure containing four factors and 15 items, including *digital skills*, *genre awareness*, *language use*, and *cohesion of modes*. To establish external construct validity, correlation analyses were conducted to explore the relationship between DMC competence and different components of L2 proficiency, i.e., reading, listening, speaking, and writing. The findings indicated significant correlations between DMC competence and overall L2 proficiency, as well as specific components, i.e., reading, speaking, and writing. Latent growth curve modelling analysis further supported the external construct validity by demonstrating that DMC competence co-developed with L2 monomodal writing competence. Interviews with students provided insights into the consequential construct validity of the DMC competence scale. Students reported that using the scale positively impacted their print-based L2 writing competence. It encouraged them to focus on aspects of writing that were applicable to both DMC and traditional writing, enhanced their understanding of what writing is and how to learn to write, and motivated them to engage in self-monitoring, self-assessment, and self-revision of monomodal texts.

The scale was applied in a DMC project as a self- and peer-assessment tool. Data from student interviews, classroom observations, and document analyses showed that the L2 student DMC competence scale played a pivotal role in students' self-assessment processes: It was the primary source of *determining performance criteria*, and could be used to generate external feedback in *self-directed feedback seeking*, and guide students' *self-reflection* and *taking action*. The scale was also useful in the peer-feedback processes: Students drew on the scale to seek and provide peer feedback, and combined the use of the scale and exemplars to maximize the learning potential of DMC peer assessment.

How does this book contribute to research and practice?

The present study makes significant contributions to several areas of research, including DMC, L2 writing assessment, scale validation and use, and assessment as learning (AaL). The study stands as a pioneering initiative in establishing a theoretical framework to understand DMC competence. By taking an emic approach, it addresses the research gap related to the ill-defined nature of DMC competence. This theoretical foundation sheds light on what constitutes L2 student DMC competence and adds to the understanding of how students engage with DMC tasks.

The book offers an exemplar for assessing technology-enhanced L2 writing tasks, setting an example for educators and researchers in similar contexts. It underscores the potential for technology to mediate and enhance students' learning experiences in writing. This approach encourages teachers to consider technology as a valuable tool in supporting students' writing development. It also contributes to changing the prevailing deficit view of L2 writers as disadvantaged compared to their L1 counterparts. Instead of evaluating L2 writers against the yardstick of L1 writers, this book advocates for a focus on understanding L2 writers as meaning makers who bring their own linguistic and non-linguistic repertoires to the writing process. This shift in perspective highlights the unique features, identities, and

Conclusion 109

voices of L2 writers, paving the way for more research into how they utilize their prior knowledge, express their identities, and make their meanings.

This book also explores the connection between DMC competence and L2 proficiency and discovers a robust correlation between DMC competence, L2 writing, and L2 speaking. This helps alleviate concerns among teachers that DMC might detract from students' language-acquisition endeavours. In addition, this research aids in advancing the design of integrated writing tasks, specifically those involving writing-to-speaking and speaking-to-writing—areas that have hitherto lacked adequate attention in the realm of language assessment.

Furthermore, this study makes a novel contribution to DMC assessment by creating and validating a DMC competence scale. Existing scales for DMC assessment lack consistency and comprehensive criteria, posing challenges to accurately evaluating students' levels of DMC competence, as well as their strengths and weaknesses in this area. This study gathers evidence pertaining to the scale's structural, external, and consequential construct validity, thereby substantiating the claim that this instrument ensures a valid interpretation and effective utilization of measurement outcomes. Researchers and educators can use this scale to assess the critical dimensions of DMC competence, providing a comprehensive view of students' DMC competence levels, gathering authentic learning evidence from students' participation in DMC projects, pinpointing areas for improvement, and evaluating the impact of teachers' innovative DMC interventions in the classroom. Teachers can utilize this scale to offer descriptive and diagnostic feedback to guide students in their DMC projects and highlight the value of assessment in fostering cooperative and participatory learning.

Lastly, self-assessment, which is at the core of AaL, has garnered significant attention from researchers and educators. This study serves as an example of implementing self-assessment in DMC projects, opening up opportunities for students to assess their own narration and writing skills. It contributes to the body of literature on self-assessment and AaL by demonstrating that the potential for learning through self-assessment can be maximized in technology-enhanced L2 writing tasks. The use of the L2 student DMC competence scale in students' self-assessment highlights the crucial role of scales in guiding the micro-level processes of students' self-assessment. Moreover, this study stands out as one of the initial attempts to apply a student self-assessment model from general education to the realm of L2 writing.

What can researchers take from this book?

The current study has significant implications for DMC research. It represents a departure from the previously elusive conceptualization of DMC competence by shedding light on the construct of L2 student DMC competence. Moreover, it offers a valid and reliable instrument for researchers aiming to measure L2 students' DMC competence. Further empirical studies are encouraged to validate the L2 student DMC competence model established in this study within various L2 contexts, such as Hong Kong, Macau, and Taiwan. Additionally, the development of scales for grading students' DMC samples is essential. Consequently, research on scale development and validation can be pursued using statistical methods like Many-facet Rasch Measurement, factor analysis, and generalization analysis, as well as qualitative approaches such as interviews and think-aloud protocols. Considering the complexity of DMC competence, the inclusion and analysis of various DMC genres, including memes, web pages, graphic novels, and PowerPoint presentations, among others, can refine the L2 student DMC competence model.

Researchers are recommended to undertake quantitative studies to scrutinize the relationship between DMC competence and other variables, factors influencing the development of DMC competence, and the developmental trajectories of this competence. Experimental and quasi-experimental studies are encouraged to probe the impact of various types of interventions. Latent profile analysis (LPA) can be performed to discern heterogeneous patterns of L2 student DMC competence levels.

Qualitative studies are also warranted, with teachers conducting autoethnography research to examine their own experiences and challenges in teaching and assessing DMC competence. This includes their professional development and the development of assessment literacy in implementing DMC projects, along with the identification of factors influencing their teaching and assessment practices. Furthermore, longitudinal case studies can provide valuable insights into students' development of DMC competence. Exploring students' perceptions and experiences as they develop DMC competence is also essential to advance our understanding of DMC competence development.

Conclusion 111

What can teachers and students take from this book?

The clarification of L2 student DMC competence elucidates the learning objectives and success criteria of DMC. Consequently, L2 writing instructors across all levels can better structure their classroom activities to target these specific aspects of DMC competence. For instance, to nurture students' awareness of different genres, teachers can assign tasks involving various genres of DMC works, like video essays, documentaries, digital storytelling, advertisements, web pages, and memes, and analyze the features of DMC works of differing genres with students. L2 teachers can adapt the L2 student DMC competence scale for assessing students' DMC projects. They can integrate AaL into their teaching methods and encourage students to utilize the scale as a self- and peer-assessment tool. The L2 student DMC competence scale can also serve as a foundation for teachers when designing their assessment criteria for AaL purposes. This scale equips teachers with the necessary skills to assess students' performance in technology-enhanced L2 writing tasks, enhances their assessment proficiency, and fosters equitable classroom-based evaluation.

This study sets an example of placing students at the forefront of DMC assessment, encouraging students to exhibit more initiative, independence, critical thinking, self-confidence, and self-directed learning. It is significant to listen to students' perspectives to inform the design and evaluation of DMC tasks. For instance, students can communicate the challenges they face when participating in DMC projects and self-assessment to teachers, along with suggestions for refining the instruction and evaluation of DMC projects.

The descriptors outlined in the scale highlight essential skills relevant in the digital era. This could potentially capture the interest of L2 curriculum developers, prompting them to integrate DMC competence into their curricula as a fundamental instructional element to enhance L2 students' digital writing skills, rather than treating it as an optional add-on.

How can we move forward?

We acknowledge the presence of certain limitations in the book. Firstly, it predominantly focuses on the video essay genre, and future research should include analysis of various genres to refine the model to accommodate different DMC projects. Secondly, the book concentrates on groups that produced outstanding DMC works to gain insights into the DMC competence employed in crafting DMC works. However, of note is that groups that produced less successful DMC works could also provide valuable information by sharing their struggles and challenges, which would contribute to a deeper understanding of the concept of DMC competence. Therefore, future research should involve participants with diverse levels of DMC competence to elucidate their DMC competence more comprehensively. Thirdly, the sample size is relatively small, comprising solely first-year university students with less advanced L2 proficiency. Therefore, future research should aim for a larger sample size, including more advanced L2 students. Fourthly, this scale was developed within a specific context, and caution needs to be taken when attempting to generalize the findings. Future studies might consider recruiting participants from various L2 contexts to enhance the generalization of the findings. Last but not the least, this book focuses on the utilization of the L2 student DMC competence scale in students' DMC self-assessment processes, and more attention is warranted on the use of the scale in students' peer-assessment processes in future studies.

Concluding remarks

This study has presented a four-factor 15-item L2 student DMC competence scale, including *digital skills*, *genre awareness*, *language use*, and *cohesion of modes*, demonstrating strong structural, external, and consequential construct validity. This scale was employed as a tool to guide students' DMC self- and peer-assessment practices.

This research sheds light on the construct of L2 student DMC competence, addressing the need for the assessment of DMC competence and offering guidance for teachers in assessing DMC projects. Furthermore, it contributes to the field of L2 writing research by embracing multimodality and emphasizing the process of meaning making. The clarification of this construct facilitates the integration of DMC competence into L2 curricula. With its validation, the scale can be employed by researchers to gauge students' levels of DMC competence, identify valid indicators of learning through participation in DMC projects, and explore its relationships with other relevant variables. Furthermore, students' utilization of this scale for DMC self- and peer assessment provides valuable insights into the implementation of AaL in technology-enhanced L2 writing tasks.

Suggested key reading materials

Deng, Y., Liu, D., & Feng, D. (2023). Students' perceptions of peer review for assessing digital multimodal composing: The case of a discipline-specific English course. *Assessment & Evaluation in Higher Education*. Advanced online publication.

Hafner, C. A., & Ho, W. Y. J. (2020). Assessing digital multimodal composing in second language writing: Towards a process-based model. *Journal of Second Language Writing, 47*, 100710.

Hung, H.-T., Chiu, Y.-C. J., & Yeh, H.-C. (2012). Multimodal assessment of and for learning: A theory-driven design rubric. *British Journal of Educational Technology, 44*(3), 400–409.

Jiang, L., Yu, S., & Lee, I. (2022). Developing a genre-based model for assessing digital multimodal composing in second language writing: Integrating theory with practice. *Journal of Second Language Writing, 57*, 100869.

Kress, G. (2000). Multimodality: Challenges to thinking about language. *TESOL Quarterly, 34*(2), 337–340.

Kress, G. (2003). *Literacy in the new media age*. Routledge.

Kress, G. (2010). *Multimodality: A social semiotic approach to contemporary communication*. Routledge.

Lee, I. (2017). *Classroom writing assessment and feedback in L2 school contexts*. Springer.

Li, M. (2021). *Researching and teaching second language writing in the digital age*. Palgrave Macmillan.

McKee, H. A., & DeVoss, D. N. (Eds.). (2013). *Digital writing assessment & evaluation*. Computers and Composition Digital Press/Utah State University Press.

New London Group. (1996). A pedagogy of multiliteracies: Designing social futures. *Harvard Educational Review, 66*(1), 60–92.

Qu, W. (2017). For L2 writers, it is always the problem of the language. *Journal of Second Language Writing, 38*, 92–93.

Ryu, J., Kim, Y. A., Eum, S., Park, S., Chun, S., & Yang, S. (2022). The assessment of memes as digital multimodal composition in L2 classrooms. *Journal of Second Language Writing, 57*, 100914.

Shin, D., Cimasko, T., & Yi. Y. (2021). *Multimodal composing in K-16 ESL and EFL education*. Springer.

Smith, B. E., Pacheco, M. B., & Khorosheva, M. (2020). Emergent bilingual students and digital multimodal composition: A systematic review of research in secondary classrooms. *Reading Research Quarterly, 56*(1), 33–52.

Yi, Y., Shin, D., & Cimasko, T. (2020). Special issue: Multimodal composing in multilingual learning and teaching contexts. *Journal of Second Language Writing, 47*, 100717.

Zhang, E. D., & Yu, S. (2023a). Implementing digital multimodal composing in L2 writing instruction: A focus on developing L2 student writers. *Innovation in Language Learning and Teaching, 17*(4), 769–777.

Zhang, E. D., & Yu, S. (2023b). Conceptualizing digital multimodal composing competence in L2 classroom: A qualitative inquiry. *Computer Assisted Language Learning.* Advanced online publication.

Zhang, E. D., & Yu, S. (2023c). The development and validation of an L2 student digital multimodal composing competence scale. *Computer Assisted Language Learning.* Advanced online publication.

Zhang, M., Akoto, M., & Li, M. (2021). Digital multimodal composing in post-secondary L2 settings: A review of the empirical landscape. *Computer Assisted Language Learning, 36*(4), 694–721.

Index

Note: Page numbers in *italics* indicate figures and in **bold** indicate tables on the corresponding pages.

Accurso, K. 26–27, 31
Andrade, H. 82
assessment 111; determining performance criteria for 93–95, *95*; introduction to 90; as learning (AaL) 90; of learning (AoL) 5; peer- 90–91, **93**, 100–102; scale-referenced self- 92–93; self- **90**, 90–100, *95*, *96*, *99*; self-directed feedback seeking in 95–97, *96*; self-reflection in 97; summary and implications of 103–104; taking action after 98–100, *99*; teacher reflection on use of DMC scale in 102–103; teachers' use of L2 student DMC competence scale in 90–102
audience awareness *25*, 25–27, 77–81
Available Design 16, *16*

Barthes, R. 13–14
Brown, G. T. L. 98
Bunch, G. C. 27, 37

Campbell, D. T. 58
Chen, Y. 25
China Central Television (CCTV) 28–29, *29*
Cimasko, T. 33

cohesion of modes 31–34, *32–33*, 47, *64*, *65*, **67**, 68
combining modes 68
Comparative Fit Index (CFI) 59–61
competence, L2 DMC 16–38, *17*, 107–108; assessment of (*see* assessment); cohesion of modes in 31–34, *32–33*, 47, *64*, *65*, **67**, 68; creativity in 27–29, *27–29*, 35, 47; data on 19–20; delivery in 30–31, 47; development of model of 18–22, *19*; digital skills in 30, 47, 65, *65*, **67**, *67*, 93–94, 101–102; dimensions of 22–38; genre awareness in 23–27, *25–26*, 35, 36, 38, 46–47, *64*, *66*, **67**, 68; identity expression in 34–35, *35*, 47; implications of model on 38–39; language use in 36–37, 47, *64*, *66*, **67**, 68; organization in 37–38, 47; research directions for 110; scale for (*see* scale, L2 DMC competence); scale validation for (*see* validation, L2 DMC scale); Student Focus Group Interview Protocol 44; utilization of multiple modes in 22–23, *22–23*, 46
confirmatory factor analysis (CFA) 58; structural construct validity and 59–68, *60*, *62–67*, **63**, **67**

consequential construct validity 74–82, **75**, *77–78*, *80*
Cook, T. D. 58
correlation analysis 69–71, **70**
COVID-19 pandemic 34
creativity 27–29, *27–29*, 35, 47; correlation with genre awareness 60–61
Cronbach's alpha 61, 65
Cumming, A. 82

delivery 30–31, 47
Design 16, *16*
digital multimodal composing (DMC) 1–5; assessment of competence in (*see* scale, L2 DMC competence); conceptualizing and modeling L2 student competence in 16–38, *17*; future of 111–112; introduction to 12–13; multiliteracies in 15–16, *16*; multimodality and 13–15; theoretical rationale for 13–16, 108–110
digital skills 30, 47, 65, *65*, **67**, *67*; peer feedback on 101–102; performance criteria of 93–94
dubbing 67–68
Dzekoe, R. 3

Elola, I. 4, 29, 35
Embretson, S. 58
external construct validity 69–74, **70**, **73**

Fairclough, N. 15
Fajardo, M. F. 3
feedback 95–97, *96*
Fiske, D. W. 58

generative artificial intelligence (GAI) 1–2
genre awareness 23–27, *25–26*, 35, 36, 38, 46–47, *64*, *66*, **67**, 68; correlation with creativity 60–61
Guan, X. Y. 25

Hafner, C. A. 14, 23, 27, 33–35, 37
Ho, W. Y. J. 23, 35

Hung, H. T. 3
Hutcheson, G. 49

identity expression 34–35, *35*, 47

Jiang, L. 18, 23, 30
Jones, R. H. 14

Kaiser, H. F. 49
Kaiser-Meyer-Olkin (KMO) measure of sampling adequacy 49
Kim, Y. 4, 35
King, N. 25, 29
Kloepfer, R. 14
Kress, G. 13, 22, 32

language use 36–37, 47, *64*, *66*, **67**, 68
latent growth curve modelling (LGCM) 58, 71–74, **73**
Lee, I. 82, 90, 92
Lee, S.Y. 3
Lennon, R. T. 58
Liang, M. Y. 31
Liaw, M. 26–27, 31
Linacre, J. 62
literacy 15
Loevinger, J. 58

Many-facet Rasch Measurement (MFRM) 61–62
Messick, S. 57, 58
Min, H. T. 92
modes 13
multiliteracies in digital multimodal composing (DMC) 15–16, *16*
multimodality of digital multimodal composing (DMC) 13–15

"New Horizon College English" 18
New London Group 15–16, 22, 27, 29, 34

O'Halloran, K. 13
organization 37–38, 47
Orsmond, P. 82
Oskoz, A. 4, 29, 35

Park, J. H. 29, 33
peer-assessment 90–91, **93**;
  scale-referenced 100–102
performance criteria 93–95, *95*

Redesigned, the 16, *16*
relay 14
Ren, W. 18, 30
Root-Mean-Square Error of Approximation (RMSEA) 59, 61
root mean square residual (RMR) 60
Ryu, J. 4, 68

scale, L2 DMC competence:
  analyzing items in 49–52, **52–54**;
  constructing items in 47–49;
  defining the construct in 46–47;
  development of 45, *46*; final version of **52–54**, **63**; first version of **50–51**; introduction to 45; summary and implications of 54–55; teacher reflection on use of 102–103; validation of (*see* validation, L2 DMC scale)
scale-referenced peer assessment 100–102
scale-referenced self-assessment 92–100
self-assessment **90**, 90–91;
  determining performance criteria for 93–95, *95*; scale-referenced 92–93; self-directed feedback seeking and 95–97, *96*; self-reflection and 97; taking action after 98–100, *99*
self-directed feedback seeking 95–97, *96*
self-reflection 97

semiotic modes 13–15
Shin, D. 33
Shulman, L. S. 58
Smith, B. 13
Smith, B. E. 25, 37
Sofroniou, N. 49
Standardized Root-Mean-Square Residual (SRMR) 60–61
structural construct validity 59–68, *60*, *62–67*, **63**, **67**

Tardy, C. 37
transduction 14–15
Tucker-Lewis Index (TLI) 59, 61

Unsworth, L. 14
utilization of multiple modes 22–23, *22–23*, 46

validation, L2 DMC scale:
  consequential construct validity 74–82, **75**, *77–78*, *80*; dimensions of validity and 58; external construct validity 69–74, **70**, **73**; introduction to 57–58; structural construct validity 59–68, *60*, *62–67*, **63**, **67**

Wechat 59
Wiggins, G. 82
Willett, K. 27, 37

Xiang, X. 92

Yan, Z. 98
Yeh, H. C. 27, 31
Yin, R. K. 19–20

Zheng, S. 18

For Product Safety Concerns and Information please contact our EU representative GPSR@taylorandfrancis.com
Taylor & Francis Verlag GmbH, Kaufingerstraße 24, 80331 München, Germany

www.ingramcontent.com/pod-product-compliance
Lightning Source LLC
Chambersburg PA
CBHW051753230426
43670CB00012B/2265